Doesn't Anybody Hear My Cry?

Doesn't Anybody Hear My Cry?

The autobiography of
RUBY ADAMS

(As dictated to and edited by Lois A. Hamilton)

XULON PRESS

Xulon Press
2301 Lucien Way #415
Maitland, FL 32751
407.339.4217
www.xulonpress.com

© 2023 by Ruby Adams

All rights reserved solely by the author. The author guarantees all contents are original and do not infringe upon the legal rights of any other person or work. No part of this book may be reproduced in any form without the permission of the author. The views expressed in this book are not necessarily those of the publisher.

Due to the changing nature of the Internet, if there are any web addresses, links, or URLs included in this manuscript, these may have been altered and may no longer be accessible. The views and opinions shared in this book belong solely to the author and do not necessarily reflect those of the publisher. The publisher therefore disclaims responsibility for the views or opinions expressed within the work.

Unless otherwise indicated, Scripture quotations taken from the King James Version (KJV) – *public domain.*

Paperback ISBN-13: 978-1-6628-2358-9
Ebook ISBN-13: 978-1-6628-2359-6

Dedication

I would like to dedicate this book to my grandchildren and my great-grandchildren.

Foreword

When I was first asked to type this book for Ruby, I had no idea that Mrs. Adams had so many inspirational messages for you as a reader. You see, I had met her through a friend during the 1980's, but she did not reveal to me that she was in the process of learning how to read until thirteen years later. At that time, she also said that she was working on learning the basic mathematical operations at the elementary level. Even though she did not know her multiplication and division tables, she was enthusiastically working toward getting a G.E.D.

Because I was a full-time elementary school teacher at the time, I almost turned down her request — due to lack of time on my part more than anything else. However, I finally decided to do it because I felt the Lord tugging at my heart to help her with her project. As we progressed through her story, we became very good friends and I am now very glad that I listened to the Lord's promptings. Ruby is just bursting forth with stories about what her life was like before she was a Christian and how it changed after she answered Christ's calling.

Ruby has stated that she had felt that it was the Lord's leading which brought me to her front door one dark rainy night in 1993 as an answer to her prayer for help. We had not seen much of each other since the Lord had brought us together in 1988. After listening to many of her trials and tribulations, I thought about how the Lord had brought her through life in spite of herself at times. I listened to how He has been walking with her since she has asked Jesus into her heart. I realized how her complete attitude had changed from that of "crying out in despair for help" to that of "the Lord will take care of me and 'even carry me' when necessary," so I accepted the mission, She now genuinely loves all of the people around her as Christ loved the world and I truly believe that you, too, can identify with some, if not many, of the situations in which she has found herself during her life.

I also believe that you may be truly inspired by the various parts of God's Word which have enabled her to live her life for the Lord. It is her prayer that her life story may bring many people to the realization that their cries for help are heard by the Lord who loves everyone — each and every person — no matter what their lifestyle may be.

Ruby and I praise and thank the Lord for letting us be His humble servants and His instruments as we bring her story to you. We pray that it helps the reader understand that, no matter how far we may be from Christ, He still hears our cries and always brings us even closer to Him. We also pray that, through her life story and the parts of His Word which may be brought to mind, many readers may come to know Christ as their Savior and Lord. It is also our prayer that every reader maybe even you — may have a closer relationship with Him. May each reader learn to walk with Him more closely each day.

Lois A Hamilton

Introduction

When I first met Ruby Adams, I knew that she was a treasure from the south not just because of her hospitable personality (because most Southerners that I know are quite hospitable) — but because of her smile, the way she walked and the way she talked, among other things. (These are things that most Southerners, especially black folks, cannot disguise no matter how hard they try — and the more they try, the more unconvincing they appear to be.)

We first met at a church function. As Ruby has done all of her life she was serving someone else; making my family feel welcome. I thought to myself, as I watched her, "This woman probably has a story packed away somewhere, just like my mother." I was immediately drawn to her, although it was not my intention to get close to anyone in this little town of Elmira, New York.

A few months passed before I saw Ruby again. This time was no different from the last. It seemed as though her bubbly spirit resumed from where it had left off the last time I had seen her. Ruby invited my family over to her house for lunch that Sabbath afternoon. As we followed "Uncle Lloyd," Ruby's husband, my husband and I commented on Ruby's Spirit-filled personality.

"Uncle Lloyd" drove slowly to get home, but we finally made it to the house. The porch had a lot to say about Ruby's personality as well. It was laid out like I remember my grandmother's house — couches and chairs taking up nearly every inch of space, inviting the weary traveler to come, sit, and relax. The setting brought back so many childhood memories for me. It also prepared my mind for what I expected to see once we graced the doors of the "Adams Castle". But, once I entered the front door, my imaginary picture had to be altered somewhat.

The woodwork caught my eyes first, so I did not focus my attention on the masterpiece that Ruby had created with her Furniture. It was not until after I caressed the woodwork, especially the columns that led from the living room to the sitting room, that I finally realized the "country" setting that Ruby had held onto from the South. The house was magnificent! In my estimation and taste, it was too over furnished to be appreciated, but this was (and still is) Ruby. Everywhere I looked, I saw the stories she told through her interior decorations. Everything was precious to her, and she proved it by displaying it.

I thought back to when I was young and how I knew my own mom would have felt right at home here. Anybody would. The only differences in our home in

Mississippi were the colors and the style of the furniture. Ruby's was very modern and seemed out of place in this house, but I saw my mother's ideas and arrangement written all over Ruby's house. I knew where everything was! Traditionally, Southern folks have the same organizational traits, and Ruby had not changed. I really felt at home right away.

During our conversation that Sabbath, I learned that Ruby and "Uncle Lloyd" owned the house, which surprised me — not because I didn't think that it was possible, but because of their ages and the length of their marriage, You see, "I Uncle Lloyd" was in his early seventies, Ruby was in her late forties at the time, and they had not been married very long.

"Such a big house for two people!" I thought to myself, looking at the beams in the ceiling. My thoughts must have spilled out of my expression because Ruby said, "I guess you must be wonderin' what Uncle Lloyd and I are doing with this big house!" I was somewhat embarrassed, but felt at ease after she put her arms around me and told me, "That's okay"…And I knew she meant it. About that time, Ruby yelled upstairs to tell everyone to come eat.

"Oh, her family lives here, "I said to myself. I discovered that I had guessed wrong again after I saw all of the different types of people, mostly white, gracing the staircase.

"This is my family," Ruby said in a dragging Southern tone. I had learned from the last embarrassing moment not to say anything, Ruby, again reading my expression, explained what these people were doing in her house. "I've been taking care of people since I was a child," Ruby responded. "These are Psych Center' patients." I acknowledged to myself how much patience a job like this must take, admitting that I could never do it. Ruby had been taking care of the emotionally and mentally disabled since she was seventeen years old. She had worked at various nursing homes in New York City.

"You'd really have to love this kind of work to do it twenty four hours a day," I said to Ruby,

"I enjoy it," Ruby said to me, smiling. She had opened the "room and boarding house" for psychiatric patients in 1980. She later took in some elderly patients.

After learning this about Ruby, I assumed that she was educated and certified, although I did not assume this until about fifteen years ago — five years after I met Ruby.

Everyone knew 107 Grove Street in Elmira, New York, as the busiest house in town. Whenever anyone decided to pop in, Ruby and "Uncle Lloyd" would be home. The doors were always close because she was like a mother to me,

One day, I came over to talk to Ruby.

"She's not here," Uncle Lloyd told me.

Surprised, I asked, "Where is she? At the grocery store?" "She ain't here. She gone to school," Uncle Lloyd said to me in his innocent, aged, Southern dialect.

Introduction

"School?" I questioned in surprise! I looked at my watch. It was seven o'clock in the evening. Uncle Lloyd told me that Ruby had left the house thirty minutes before I had gotten there. I went into the house to search for something sweet to eat because Ruby always had some sort of dessert around the house. As I searched, I wondered to myself if I had misunderstood "Uncle Lloyd". I remembered the last time Ruby had left a message for me — and how he had gotten it mixed up.

"Are you sure she went to school?" I questioned him again.

"I'm sho," Uncle Lloyd said, laughing at my disbelief.

"Tell her to call me when she gets back," I told him.

Ruby hadn't called by nine, so I became worried and called her.

Ruby answered the phone.

"What happened? Why didn't you call me?" I asked frantically.

"Hello, Sweetie," Ruby said, calming me down at which time I apologized.

Ruby inquired as to what was wrong.

"Nothing's wrong. It's just that when I came to your house, you weren't there," I said.

"I know, Darlin'," Ruby said.

"Where were you? Uncle Lloyd said that you were in school," I replied.

"I was," Ruby said sweetly.

"What for?" I asked inquisitively.

Ruby's silence told me that she didn't want to answer, so I didn't press the issue. I could tell that she wanted to keep her secret. Perhaps she was somewhat embarrassed. I told her that I wasn't used to her not being at home whenever I stopped by. Later, Ruby felt as though she had to explain why she could not tell me about her secret, but she apologized that she couldn't. I assured her that she didn't have to tell me, or anyone else, what she wanted to keep to herself, and that anyone should be able to understand.

I got used to Ruby not being home whenever I dropped by unannounced. So, I started calling ahead before I went over to her house I missed not having her around and became jealous of her new-found love. Almost two years passed, and as they did, my relationship with Ruby became somewhat distant — the distance that I thought that I had wanted in the beginning. One day, I sporadically dropped by, and to my surprise, I found Ruby home. She was bubbling over as usual, so I didn't inquire as to why. I didn't quite know what to say to her. Inside, I was happy for whatever it was that made Ruby happy, but I was afraid to show Ruby my emotions. I was afraid that she would feel compelled to tell me everything.

"Aren't you happy for me?" she inquired.

I assured her that I was, but I didn't think that she believed me. Feeling the distance, Ruby explained to me that, that particular type of reaction was the reason that she didn't tell people about her going back to school. She did not want to risk being criticized by anyone.

"I'm not just 'people', I said to her. "I just assumed that our relationship was trusting enough that you'd believe that I would be happy for you."

She went on to explain that she did not have a formal education — as I had previously assumed — at which time I explained, "I didn't know that you didn't have an education. I just assumed that you did because of all the things that you're doing." (Apparently, I was not the first person to tell Ruby that. With absolutely no formal education, she was a pretty smart lady!)

Ruby had absolutely nothing to be embarrassed about, and yet she was embarrassed. What she had accomplished with such few resources was absolutely remarkable, and she had "done it without encouragement". Six months later, after Ruby and I had put this incident to rest, we somehow found ourselves talking about it again. At this point, however, she eloquently explained that she had a desire to write her life story.

She wanted to try to inspire others through the story of her life, but she was somewhat reluctant because she needed someone whom she could trust to do the writing for her. My intention was to give Ruby only the guidance that she needed. Then she gave me a look that I would only expect from my own mother. With her solemn look, and pleading voice, she made her request: to type her life story. I could not turn Ruby down, so we began our new project.

I felt, and Ruby agreed, that the Lord had brought us together. I told her that the Lord spared her life, saying, "After all that you've gone through, Ruby, it's a miracle that you have lived this long. God is the only one who could be watching over you to bring you this far in life," We both laughed!

I felt good as I looked forward to working on the new project. When I left Ruby that night, she had the joy of a little child written all over her. She thanked me over and over again. However, even though I was not able to complete the project, quite frankly, I should be thanking you, Ruby. It's been my privilege to work with you for a little while. Thank you.

Angela Martin

Overview

This is an autobiography about a black lady, Ruby Adams, who was born in Waynesboro, Georgia, She grew up on a cotton plantation. She began learning what it was like to work hard to earn a living at the early age of five. However, hard work for her was not by choice, but by force. Parts of the story tells about her life in the deep south. There are parts of her life history which include being gang raped, and then later she tells about being attacked by a white man in broad daylight. This all happened at a very early age.

In her story, she tells about her moves to Elmira, New York, to New York City, and back to Elmira, and she tells about all of the hardships she had to endure with members of her family, with her spouses, and with her friends.

The point of the book is to share how God lead her through her life, and how He can lead others as well, through their lives if they will only let Him. He lead her every step of the way, even though she didn't understand His will for her life at the time. She also shares how "…all things work together for good to them that love God, to them who are the called according to His Purpose." (Romans 8:28).

Her story shows how she truly wondered if God was really there. After accepting Christ as her Savior, she tells of her backsliding, doubts, and her sinful ways. But, she tells her readers that the Lord made it possible for her to succeed in life in spite of her lack of a formal education due to her childhood circumstances on the plantation and the various other happenings in her lifetime. She tells how she succeeded strictly because of the Grace of God.

After having listened to her incredible life story, I know it has to be God who leads in her life. There's no other way that one person could endure so many different problems — starting at such a young age — any other way. The Lord brought her through all of her trials and tests and polished her like a precious gem so she could shine like a beacon, bringing the story of salvation to others each step of the way. At this point in her life, all I can hear from her lips is thankfulness for God's faithfulness and mercy. She tries to glorify Him in everything that she does or says.

My Stormy Beginning

It was a dark, dreary, cold night when the Lord decided I should enter this world — about four or five o'clock in the morning on February 16, 1938. I was the first born, living, child to Henry and Willie Mae Graham who lived on a farm in Waynesboro, Georgia, in the deep, deep South. We lived in a two-room shack on a farm called the Francis Kate Place. Of course, if I had known then what I had found out by the time I was six years old, I probably would have changed my mind about being born – If I had a choice in the matter.

You see, when I was five years old, I had to go out into the cotton fields for the first time. In the hot summer weather, I helped chop (hoe) cotton. Sometimes the temperatures would be up to over 100 degrees Fahrenheit, Man alive, it was hot!! The cotton, when it was in full bloom, was very pretty. I just loved to look out over those beautiful green fields and gaze at the gorgeous soft fluffy white cotton blossoms. Even though it looked so beautiful in early summer, by the time we picked the cotton in the fall, it was very hard work and we worked our fingers to the bone. It didn't take long before I felt like an older person. All of us, even the older folks, seemed to age faster because of what we were made to do. Even now, I can see myself in my mind's eye, as a little six-year-old child out there in the simmering heat trying my best to pick cotton off of bushes that were bigger than me. I'd have to reach a long way into the cotton bush and I'd get all scratched up from those old dry brown cotton plants.

The hardest part of living on that plantation was that I had to get up r-e-a-l early every morning, about five o'clock, because I had to feed the animals before we all went to the cotton fields. It was about that time that I thought I knew beyond a doubt what "hard work" was really like. As you can see, I was taught to go out and earn an honest living very early in life.

One day when my mother and father had to go out and work in the fields, they decided, even though I was only six and a half years old, that I had to stay "home" to baby-sit my sister and my brother. This was the first time they had had to do that, but there wasn't anybody else to help them. As I look back, I think that it was then that "my troubles' really started" because my brother Pete was only four years old and my sister Osie was only two. As I tried to do my best. I thought, "I can't do this by myself. I need help! I'm only a little girl! Help!! Doesn't anybody hear my cry?"

My father never felt that Pete was really his son because of what people had said about my mother and what she had been doing with other men while he was away from home for a little while. You see, my folks were separated for a little while. Because of the way he felt, he sent Pete to live with my Grandmother Della and my Grandfather Buster. Pete lived there with them for the rest of his childhood at my grandmother's advice. This really crushed my mother because she couldn't actually understand why my father would ship Pete out "just because of some rumor." But, even though Pete and I were separated, my mother and I would go see him every Sunday, My Grandmother Della was a very compassionate woman, so she tried to help our family with the situation to the best of her ability.

Let me pause here for a moment and tell you a little about my mother's parents:

Over the years my Grandmother Della told me true stories about how she was born to Sam and Liza Kline. She told me that her mother, my Great-grandmother Liza, was sold into slavery when she was only twelve years old to a doctor and his wife. Grandma Della said that the doctor was good to her mother. She said that he took Liza on his "house calls" taught her how to care for the sick, and showed her how to deliver babies on his plantation, so she became an excellent midwife. Grandma said that her mother intended to deliver me, but she died two months before I was born. Unfortunately, she did not live long enough to see any of Grandma Della's grandchildren born.

As my Great-Grandmother Liza grew up on the doctor's plantation in Vidette, Georgia, which was about thirteen miles west of Waynesboro, she met Sam Kline who was also a slave. She was fourteen years of age and Sam was eighteen when they got married. Out of that union there were five girls and three boys -eight children – My Grandmother Della and seven others. As Great-Grandfather Sam and Great-grandmother Liza, and eventually their whole family, were shipped from plantation to plantation, they lived in some of the most run-down shacks I ever heard about. Grandmother Della told me that her parents as well as her brothers, sisters, and herself had to eat and to drink from a hog trough like the pigs.

My Grandmother Della also grew up and got married at the age of fourteen just like her mother had done. She married my Grandfather Buster Vaughn, who, like my Great-grandfather Sam, was also eighteen. They, too, had eight children.

But, to marry Grandma, Grandpa "ran away from home" which had been in Norfolk, Virginia. One starry night he just told his parents that he was going to go work on a place where they "skin cows" which was much like a butcher shop in those days.

To make a long story shorter, the way my Grandmother Della told it to us, "My mother (my Great-grandmother Liza) told me that I (Della) was too young to get married, but that didn't stop your Grandfather Buster."

To everyone's surprise, he came by her house one night with a mule pulling an Old rugged green wagon and stole my Grandmother Della out through the window while everyone else was sleeping. They eloped to Mrs. Francis Kate's place near Midville, Georgia, about fifteen miles south of Vidette, and became her servants. It was there that they settled down to "farm" and to raise their family. All of their children and grandchildren were born and raised there. It was unusual for the whole family to stay in one place that long. Fortunately, Grandma Della had been taught by my great-grandmother how to care for the women on the plantation, so she, too, became a great midwife, she delivered many babies on the plantation and she assisted in the delivery of several of her grandchildren, but I wasn't one of them.

They stayed there until 1961 when my Aunt Mattie earned enough money to build a small house for them in Waynesboro, Georgia. She moved them from the farm to the small house because she realized they were getting too old to "farm" any more. She was very protective of my grandparents. She was like the backbone of the family. They stayed there until the Lord called them to their rest. My Grandmother Della was eighty-four and my Grandfather Buster was eighty-six years old when they were laid to rest. They were both beautiful Christian people. Praise God!!

I must get back to my own life story though: As I grew up, from the time of my first experience of taking care of my sisters and brothers, little did I know that much of my life was going to be such a hard struggle — even to this day— but, in a different way.

As I look back I realize, though, that *Romans 8:28* has been very true throughout my life, Even though I did not know God like I do now, He worked <u>everything</u> together for good. God used all of my cries for help, my doubts, my troubles, my questions, my problems, my sins, my backsliding, or whatever my circumstances were at various times, He worked them all together for "good" so that I could bring more glory to His name in these later years of my life.

There were even times that I felt like, maybe, I should have been born to different parents. "Maybe things would have been a little bit better for me that way," I thought. But I didn't realize how bad "things" were going to get before I would have a real peace in my heart — a peace that no worldly person can know before they ask Christ to be their Savior.

The reason that I felt that way about my parents so early in my life was because my mother had four more children after Pete and Osie. When I turned eight, Henry was born. By the time I was ten, she had Willie. When I was twelve, Rosie was born and, by the time I was fourteen, my mother had her last child, Bobby. My troubles really began by the time I was almost sixteen. I just thought, I had had troubles before, but circumstances got worse. "Oh, doesn't anybody hear my cry?" I wondered.

During my early childhood, I found myself wondering, "Why? Just why couldn't I have been born to someone else? Why?"

You see, I really thought my parents didn't care about me at all!! I thought they didn't even know how! Oh, how I wanted them to love and to care about me! But, I found myself thinking, "After all, who is doing all the work — me. And, who is always just laying around?"

The answer to the last question certainly wasn't, "Me." I felt like I was doing everything and that my folks weren't doing much of anything at all to help.

I'd find myself crying out for help, down deep in my heart "Doesn't anybody hear me?

HELP! Is there anybody out there?"

"Why couldn't I be like my friend, Annie Willie?" I would wonder. Then my mind would drift off, thinking about Annie, thoughts such as: "After all, she got to play and she got to go to school. She got to do everything!" And boy, did she flaunt it! Whenever she was around, she'd remind me of the things she could do.

Sometimes she would do it verbally and at other times, she did it physically by pointing out the tattered dress that I had to wear, or maybe by making fun of something else such as my run-down white and brown shoes with the curled up toes. I'll never forget those shoes, either. Her abuse got so bad that I couldn't stand to see her coming toward me! She was always putting me down! Each time I saw her I wondered in anguish, "Oh, doesn't anybody hear my cry….Anybody? ANYBODY AT ALL??

I really felt robbed of my childhood because I always had to fill in where my mother was missing! I had to take care of my three brothers and two sisters! That, by itself, doesn't sound too troublesome. However, some of them were almost my age! I had to do everything for all of them just like my mother and my father should have done, if they were taking care of them. I had to make meals for them beginning somewhere around the time each of them turned one year old.

I had to change "didees". I had to put them down for a nap. But, that wasn't the whole story! If I wasn't taking care of my brothers and sisters, I had to take my mother's place in the cotton fields! The only thing I knew was work, work, work, and more more! I never had time to play. I wondered, "Is this my purpose in life? Is this all I'll ever do? Will I ever be able to enjoy life? Enjoy life! What does that mean? Will I always have to work? After all, I am only a child!

Sometimes I don't know what I really want, but I need help. I need love! Help! Doesn't anybody hear my cry?"

I said, "Oh, God, if work is my purpose in life, take me away! I don't want this job!"

Because I didn't know Christ as my Savior at that point in my life, I didn't realize that I had used the Lord's name in vain that day. All I really knew was that I was extremely frustrated and very angry.

Something else that I didn't realize was that God was "workin' on me". He was the potter and I was the clay even though I didn't realize it. He had begun making me into a person who would be able to serve other people better and bring more glory to His Name as I reach out to others now. He wanted me to have a "servant's heart" so that I would be humble and serve them, and do everything for them "as if I was doing it for Him" after I asked him into my heart, and asked Him to be my Lord and Savior. But it was going to be a long, long, hard road full of all sorts of trials, troubles, and tribulations before I would finally really submit myself to the Lord.

Looking back, my biggest problem was that I just didn't know anything about God or how to say the "sinner's prayer". If I had, I could have come to know Him sooner. If I had, He could have walked close to me, holding my hand so I wouldn't have had to struggle so hard through life. If I had, He would have even carried me through the roughest waters of life during my toughest trials. If I had, He would have healed my broken heart and bound up my wounds *(Psalm 147-3)*. If I had, He would have been with me at all times *(Matthew 28:20)*. If I had, He would have "parted the sea" for me as He did for the Israelites in *Exodus 14*. Also God would have given me a way to escape the troubles which I had experienced just as He did for the Corinthian believers when He said that He would not let them be tempted beyond what they could bear, but that if they were tempted, He would provide a way of escape *(1 Corinthians 10:13)*. If I had, I would have always been able to cast all of my cares upon Him *(I Peter 5:7)*.

But, in the beginning, I really felt like an extremely tiny voice crying out in the wilderness, "Help!! Doesn't anybody hear me? Isn't there anybody out there? Is there a God? If there is, can He hear me? I need help! Doesn't ANYBODY hear my cry?"

I felt like I was all alone and that no one knew anything about my depressing problems, or if they did, they couldn't or wouldn't do anything about them. "After all," I thought, "Nobody has ever experienced situations as bad as mine!" How wrong was I, but this was my mindset not only as a child but as a person that had not fully accepted Christ in their life.

I felt much like the Psalmist in Psalms 130: 1 as he cried out to the Lord, asking the Lord to "hear his voice" However, at the beginning of my deepest despair, I did not know that there was a God, let alone a living God, who could really answer my prayers or my pleas for help. During my early childhood I had heard a lot about God, but I really didn't truly know Him, so I didn't have any idea that God cared about anybody at all, especially me.

Now , I know that He cared so much for me that He sent His only Son to earth to die on the cross for me, and for everyone else who will believe in Him, so that we may have eternal life (John 3:16). I know, too, that God was the only One who could part the many deep waters of my life for me so that I would eventually be able to live a peaceful life as I walk through my life on earth with Him. Yes, I still have my occasional trials, but I have learned that Jesus can give me a "real peace in my heart," a peace beyond all understanding *(Philippians 4:7),* about anything and everything.

For instance, later in my life, He gave me a burden for missionary work. I didn't know when, where, or how He was going to bring this about, but I put my trust in Him and He provided a house as well as the volunteers, the money, and the equipment with which to fix it up. I didn't have to borrow any money. Everything was provided once I gave the project to Him.

He can give everyone on Earth that same kind of peace if, and only if, they will just open their hearts to Him. This means you, too. Yes, even you and all of your friends or family, if you will only ask Him to be your Savior.

The rest of this story is my attempt to tell you just how low a person can sink and still be able to have the Lord rescue them, You may be saying to yourself, "I've done so many things wrong that there's no way God would want anything to do with me. "

But, my friend, after you read my life story, I pray that you'll be saying to yourself, "If the Lord will rescue Ruby, and eventually take her to be with Him in Heaven, then maybe, JUST

MAYBE, He'll rescue me, too. Maybe you'll even say something like, "Now that I know how Ruby is no longer separated from God, I want to ask Him to be my Savior and Lord, too."

But, please, friend, don't wait any longer because you don't know what will happen tomorrow, just as I never know what will happen from day to day. I do know, though, that whatever happens in my life, I will thank God for it. I also know that, if He were to come back while I am writing this book, I will be with Him. My dear reader, do you know where you will be? *(Ephesians 2:8-9, NIV)* says, "For it is by grace you (can be) saved, through faith — and this not from yourselves, it is the gift of God — not by works, so that no one can boast."

My School Days

When I was seven years old I started school in what they called the "primer grade" in an unpainted "one-room school house". The "primer grade" at that time in Waynesboro, Georgia, was a lot like Head start and Kindergarten in Elmira, New York, around the 1980's, except for the fact that there were about twenty children of all ages in the same room and there was only one teacher at a time teaching all of the grades. We didn't have desks. There were two big, long wooden tables at which we had to sit to do our school work. However, all I can actually remember that I really learned, though, as far as "academic subjects" are concerned, was the nursery rhymes.

I can well remember my teachers, Miss Carrie Belle Johnson and Miss Oreta Baker, though. Miss Carrie Belle always came to school looking like she was dressed to go out and work in the cotton fields. My guess is that she had to work in the fields after school, but I don't know that for sure. All I am really sure of is that sometimes when those white plantation owners needed help, they always came to our school. Whenever they did that, all of our precious learning came to a halt so that the teacher, and some of the bigger kids, could go out and work in their fields.

Before we were old enough to work in the fields ourselves, we would have to go straight home whenever the teacher left the school. She would have to go to work for the plantation owners. When we got home, instead of relaxing like most kids do today, we had to do our chores and help do whatever needed to be done for the rest of the day. When we got older, early dismissal usually meant that we would have to go home and work in the fields until the sun set and the evening came upon us. That made for a long, long day. Often, as we worked steadily, we might get a chance to quickly glance at the beautiful sunsets with various gorgeous shades ranging from orange to shades of deep red-orange colors in them. Sometimes, we could even see shades of pink, red, or purple in them.

I had a couple of secret wishes as a child. First, I often wished that I was on the other side of the sun. In my mind, I pictured myself in a beautiful city beyond the sun where little girls didn't have to slave in the fields or work hard taking care of their siblings before they were at least fourteen or fifteen years old.

Second, I wanted to get a real good education, an education like the white boys and girls could get; an education that was not interrupted by plantation owners wanting more help in the fields! However, that dream couldn't come true, either, because of the day and the age, as well as the circumstances, in which I was living at that particular time of my life. You see, I was living in the deep, deep South which made things worse, especially in the 1950's. Why? Because there were lots of troubled times for someone of my color — black.

As a thought on the side, Martin Luther King hadn't started to try to help people like us to see his "dream" of all people being equal and "Free at last, free at last, thank God Almighty, we'll be free at last…" Even after he lead the marches for the freedom for us, it didn't matter much in the deep South. The white people still had a mindset like those who had survived the Civil War one hundred years before in the nineteenth century. Black people were still treated very differently from white people; almost like slaves, the white men were not called "master," but they acted like they wanted the role back.

As I look back on my life now, I realize that the 'freedom" that Martin Luther King was talking about is a TRUE freedom only "when we follow the example of Jesus." Then, and only then, WE ARE REALLY "FREE"! I can now thank God for my ability to understand this Biblical meaning of "true freedom."

But, to get back to my story, Miss Carrie Belle did the best she could to teach us, even under those terrible trying conditions. I don't think she had much of an education, herself, though, but she did the best she could under the circumstances. The white folks just put "a live black person" in the school to teach us as much as she had been taught. They didn't care whether or not she had a college education, either. They just gave "lip-service" to fulfilling the minimum requirements set down by the state Department of Education. As far as I know, nobody from the Department of Education ever came to check on our teachers because all of the people in that Department were white, too, and the "whites" just didn't seem to care about the education of the "blacks."

So, as you can see, the white people who ran the plantations didn't really care how much we, the black people, could learn from Miss Carrie Bell. As long as we were there to work in their fields, they couldn't have cared less about what we learned, or how much we were able to learn in the short amount of time that they gave us to learn in JUST A FEW "SHORT YEARS! As I remember, I never heard anything about "college" mentioned by anybody until I left the deep South and came north to Elmira, New York,

Oh, yes, I was extremely bitter about my lack of schooling for a long time, especially when I looked around to see the big beautiful yellow school bus go by our house to pick up the white kids on the place at which we lived at the time, Those mean white kids always yelled at us, "Hey,

Nigga', we hate you!" Oh, this brings to mind a story and thought that I must share with you:

I'll never forget the time that my mother sent me through a front yard that belonged to some white people. She told me to go to their front door and to ask for some food because we didn't have any, those nasty white kids came after me just like "'mad dogs chase you when they are attacking you". They wanted to make sure that I knew that I was not supposed to come to their front door ever again.

"Go to the back door, Nigga' they'd say."

I was only about ten or eleven years old at the time. Can you imagine what this did to me? It made me feel like a person who really didn't belong to anyone anywhere. Even now, when I get a chance to travel back to the deep South these types of memories are still very much alive. It seems that many changes have taken place. Perhaps, on the surface, but I soon realize that there hasn't been very much real change taken place during these years which have gone by since that time. I can still hear the echo of the voice of the white man as he says, "Get rid of the Nigga'. He does not belong in the same territory that we belong in. Let's send them all back to Africa!"

Believe me, I am not saying that there are not good Christian white people all over the world, but it just seems like the South is so "distant", especially the deep South. I say "distant" because when most whites in the South come within view of the blacks they "clam up", especially the older generations. This does not apply so much to the younger generations because their eyes have been opened to the fact that some blacks are just as smart and just as intelligent, if not more so, than some whites.

Even I was blind to the point that I thought that my own race didn't know anything except work in the fields. I then did some research and found out that the blacks have been responsible for many things in our American culture. When I found out all of that information and my eyes were opened, I said to myself, "Where did the white race get off saying that the black race is ignorant?"

I thank God that my eyes were opened through my education and my reading of God's Word. As I read I wondered, "Do the white people read the Bible? Do they read the Word of God? If they do, they should have known that all men were created equal. I know that God brought me to that realization because of my many, many white friends with which He has blessed me with.

I really thank God, to this day, that He planted His Love in my heart because now, when I look back on those days, I can truly say that God has given me a true peace about all those unhappy circumstances which I experienced.

But, getting back to my story about school, it seemed to me that Miss Carrie Belle had some "Teacher's Pets" because, in my thoughts, she seemed to cater to some children and not to others.

For instance, I remember one time when she promised to take me to her home to spend the night. However, when that special time came, she didn't take me, Instead, she took some other girls. One of those girls was my "friend" Annie Willie. Miss Carrie Belle made me feel like I just wasn't "good enough" to be one of "her girls." I felt like she treated me like her "scrub girl." Oh, how I cried when I found out that I wouldn't be able to go to her house on that particular weekend! I quietly sobbed, "Does anybody hear my silent pleas for help? Doesn't anybody care?"

The school that I attended was the Thomas Hill School which, besides having only one room, was a long way back in the dark thick woods, just like all of the other students, we were given chores to do. You'll never believe what we had to do! Much to our dismay, we had to sweep the grounds around the school every day with a blush broom that had been made from brush from the woods. Yes, you guessed it, we were the ones who had to make the brooms. We were also responsible for going into the woods, cutting the brush and the tall weeds, and bringing it back to the school yard. If that was being "educated," that's about all I learned to do. That was about all I can remember about my "education" besides learning my nursery rhymes that I mentioned above.

It was extremely hard for me to forget about "that kind of schooling" after having to go into the woods, gather the brush and weeds, make the broom, sweep the ground, and be completely covered with dust from my head to my feet every day.

Thinking back, though, and considering how the Lord has asked us to be all kinds of servants to all people, this gathering of the brush, making of the brooms, and sweeping of the grounds was, in His eyes, a good education for me because of the ministry that He had for me, For this, I am now very thankful.

I was nine years old by the time I got to second grade. At the time of this writing, children are usually seven years old or no older than eight when they reach second grade. I can remember numbers on cards that the teacher worked with in the second grade, but since I didn't go to school every day, I don't actually remember what we were supposed to do with them. You see, by the time I returned to school after each time I had been absent, the class was learning something new. Therefore, I had to try to catch up, but I was so far behind that I couldn't understand what was being taught. Besides, the teacher never had anyone help me. SHE didn't take the time to help me, either.

It probably wouldn't have done much good, anyhow, because most of the time my mind was on what I had to do when I got home. I was always wondering how much work I would have to do. Would I have to chop wood for the fire? Would I have to stay in the house for the whole evening to "baby-sit" my sisters and brothers? Would I have to go out to the fields and work some more for my mother? Or, would they find something else, something different, for me to do?

As I remember, school was fun for a while. But, one day as I was walking the trail on my way home from school, about ten kids from school did something really bad to me! They stripped all my clothes off of me and they "got on top of me". There were about seven boys and three girls in the group.

I screamed — and screamed — and screamed, "Help! Help!! H-E-L-P!!! H-E-L-P!!!

It was only after I screamed so loud, that they left me alone and ran. I put my clothes back on and ran home as fast as I could I burst through the door and told my father what had happened. I told him that most of the kids in the group were in Mr. Robert Davis' family.

My father jumped up and quickly went over to their house to tell their papa about it, but their grandfather didn't want to listen to reason, Why? Because he didn't believe that any of the kids in his family would ever do anything like that to me, or to anybody else. Even though nothing was done about the Davis kids, I felt very proud of my father. After all, he had tried to protect me,

Mother just said that those kids didn't have much "home trainin'." She said that they were "wild little things." She also said that it was "'cause their papa and grandpapa protected them," and that "they didn't' have much respect for any other people, " After that terrible experience, my mother told me to take the paved road to go to and from school.

At first, taking the highway seemed to be a much safer way to walk to school. I would be out in the open where people could see me instead of being in the woods on a dark tree-lined narrow trail. There were also more houses on the paved road, which made it more "public". It was also a very pretty walk. As I walked along the side of the road, I could see the different colored cars as they passed me, the beautiful tall whispering pine trees, and the other pretty scenery that God had put there just for me, or so it seems, as I look back on that time in my life.

Every day on my way to school I would cross a beautiful creek of rustling crystal-clear blue-tinted water. When I reached the old wooden bridge, I always stopped to look at the abundant variety of fish which were swimming around beneath it. There were so many different sizes and kinds of fish that I often tried to count the different types that I could see as they darted this way and that. They looked like they didn't have a worry in the world as they swam around in the crystalline pool below me. As I made my way to and from school every day, I used to listen to the beautiful songs of the various birds. I especially liked their mating songs in the spring. But, no matter what time of the year it was, it seemed like my fine feathered friends were all talking just to me as I passed by, Maybe God was trying to talk to me through them to cheer me up. I certainly felt at peace as I set off for school, or as I made my way home, each day UNTIL ... it happened again!

Yes, that nightmare that scarred me in the dark trail in the deep dark woods with the boys and girls, almost happened again one day but this time it was a man in a white car. I was hopping, jumping, skipping along, and playing games as I made my way home from school one cheerful bright sunny afternoon. Suddenly, a big white car drove up next to me. I could see the big fat white man who was driving it. The first thing I knew, he quickly stopped the car! He jumped out of the car and reached for me, saying, "Come here, little Nigga' girl!"

Just as he grabbed for me, I took off through the woods trying to hold all of my belongings tightly to my chest. Whenever I would drop anything, such as my lunch pail for instance, I would hastily grab at it, hoping that I could get it on the first try because I thought I could hear him right behind me. I spotted a nearby briar patch, so I quickly darted into it. I knew I had to get away from him, no matter how I had to do it, the brush through which I was running was a large patch of briar bushes filled with thistles and thorns.

"Run, Ruby, run!" I cried to myself as I ran to and fro. As I ran through the shrubbery and the thorny brush, my legs seemed to feel each and every thorn. When I finally burst through the door of my house and got a chance to examine them closely, I could see that my legs were very badly scratched. I still have the scars on my legs today from that incident!

My tranquil cheerful trip home had been changed into a horrible nightmare in the twinkling of an eye. It was then that I discovered that taking the highway wasn't always safe, either. I have never liked white cars since that day; not even now! As I made my way home after the incident with the big fat white man, I wondered more than ever, "Doesn't anybody hear my cry?

Doesn't anybody care what happens to me? Doesn't anybody really CARE??"

To this very day, I cannot be alone in a room, or anywhere else, with a big fat white man when I am doing any kind of activity, even Christian or business activities. It really frightens me! I know that it's only by the grace of God that I'm still alive today to tell this story. It was so, "scary"!

I didn't know it then, but I now know for sure that, if he could have caught me, he would have raped me. Maybe he would have even killed me. Therefore, even now, I cringe every time I see anyone that even resembles him, even if they are smiling at me. My only thoughts were that this person was out to hurt me. I sobbed giant tears within my heart as I cried out again in my thoughts and actions. "Help! Doesn't anybody hear me? Doesn't anybody care about me?"

My time had come. I had to stay home from school many times to take care of my brothers and sisters while my mother went to the cotton fields. Later, the plantation overseer would pull us out of school whenever he needed more help in the fields, especially as we got bigger or older. Yes, you guessed it! One day, the overseer told my mother that I couldn't go back to school anymore.

So, there I was, with only a second grade education. I was to work either in the cotton fields when they needed extra help or I was to stay home to care for my younger brothers and sisters. Or, because my mother was always "sick," I would have to take her place in the fields. However, the white plantation owner, the white overseer, and the other white folks, didn't care in the least that I had no education or that I had to quit school at such an early age. Why? Because most white folks in the Deep South didn't think that black folks deserved any schooling, anyhow!

I can remember being extremely sad and crying a lot when I was told that I couldn't go back to school. Finally, one day, my grandmother told me to always do as I was told whether I wanted to do it or not.

As I look back, I think she may have been thinking about Colossians 3:20 that says, "Children, obey your parents in everything; for this pleases the Lord" or maybe it was Isaiah 41:10 that tells us "not to fear, for He is with us: do not be dismayed for I am your God. I will strengthen you and help you…" So, all I needed to do was to be obedient.

She told me that God loved all people, "blacks" and 'whites". During those times maybe she was thinking about John 3:16 (NIV) that says, 'For God so loved the world, that He gave His one and only Son that whosoever believes in Him shall not perish but have eternal life."

To get back to my story, the first time I ever heard anything about God was when Grandmother Della told me about Him. However, it was extremely hard for me to really believe that someone, anyone, had loved me that much, especially when I didn't really think that anybody at all was listening to my cries for help.

It was from about that time on that I learned to accept the idea that everything that was available for white people was NOT always available for us black folks. Going to school was one of those things! Our teachers had taught us how to cook and how to clean in school, but I wanted to learn how to read, to write, and to do arithmetic! Since I was never allowed to learn these things as a child, I forced myself to believe that I really didn't need to be educated, that education was a luxury for only white folks, and that poor people couldn't afford it, especially when having to eat was a much higher priority at the time.

But, now that I look back after I've reached and passed the age of 60, I realize that people like my grandmother and I learned to live with the outcomes of our situations as they were put upon us. We learned to live for the minute. I think that's why I have a greater appreciation for the little things in life. I believe that my Grandma Della helped me to learn to be more grateful for the smaller things that go unnoticed by so many people like good health, something to eat, and faith in our Father in heaven.

I suppose you are wondering why I talk so much more highly of my grandmother than of my mother. I believe it is because she imparted unto me much more Biblical wisdom than my mother did, even though she couldn't read. She was a very caring Christian lady. I can express in words only part of what she did for me. She had a lot of compassion for me. If needed to ask anyone a question about delicate matters like "girl talk," I could depend upon her, not my mother, to tell me the facts of life which would help me grow up to be a nice respectable young lady. I could also count on her to discuss whatever questions happened to be on my heart at the time of our various conversations.

My mother, on the other hand, seemed to turn her back on me whenever I thought I needed her the most. Sometimes she did not seem to care about my feelings, or even what I was thinking about at all, whereas my grandmother was always there and loved me tenderly, no matter what my questions or problems seemed to be. I couldn't talk to my mother like I could talk to Grandmother Della. I felt like I could open my heart to my grandmother, but I felt like I was shut out by my mother.

However, I must stop and remember that my mother was not really ready to raise a family at the time that we all arrived on the scene, especially the girls. The girls needed a special kind of love and care that she did not seem to be able to provide when it concerned more delicate "female" issues. Therefore she really didn't know how to love us as we needed to be loved. My mother also had to handle the stress which was being put on her by the white overseer whereas my grandmother was able to give her problems to the Lord and leave them there.

Now I think I know how Jesus must feel when we turn our backs on Him because He wants us to walk more closely with Him each and every day, but some of us turn our backs on Him without loving Him. He is always there, asking us to come closer, but we sometimes turn away from Him, being unable to love Him. I think this is similar to the way I felt when I thought my mother seemed to turn her back on me, seeming unable to love me with a true Christian love.

As I think back on those situations, I see where we were "persecuted, but not abandoned; struck down, but not destroyed" (II Corinthians 4:9, NIV) and we were supposed to "cast all of our anxiety on the Lord because He cares for us. (1 Peter 5:7, paraphrased). The Lord was faithful. He kept His promises, even though I didn't really "know Him at that time.

Oh, how I now praise the Lord that I was able to go back to school in Elmira, New York, at the age of 54 to get a basic academic education! I couldn't read except for a very few words until I was about nineteen, but God taught me how to read my Bible.

One day, when I was lying on my bed in 1962, I wanted to read my Bible very much. All of a sudden John 3:16, telling how much God loves me, appeared before my eyes in red letters. Since that day, I have been able to read and to comprehend my Bible. PRAISE GOD FOR THE HOLY SPIRIT WHO PROMISED TO TEACH US ALL THINGS! Now, I can read all sorts of printed materials which enable me to teach Sabbath

School, read contracts, and work with the Social Services Department of Chemung County, New York.

I am even able to dictate and proofread this story about my life. God has given me very good composition skills, but I can dictate a story easier than I can write it because I can talk faster than I can write. God has not supplied me with "spelling and penmanship abilities" as great as the "composition and dictation abilities" with which He has enabled me to write my biography. Perhaps that's because He wanted to keep me humble and let me share my stories through the God-given abilities of others as well as with my readers.

I have also learned how to figure out some problems in arithmetic, even when they involve a little bit of multiplication and division, especially if I have a calculator. The Lord has provided me with "just the right amount" of the various and sundry "correct" abilities that He knew I would need to take care of my household correctly. Isn't He MARVELOUS?? He makes no mistakes.

PRAISE the LORD!!

I know it was the Lord's grace, and only the Lord's grace, that helped me through those "lean" years of my life even though I couldn't read much. I now give Him all the praise and the glory because, as Philippians 4:13 (*NIV*) says, "I can do everything through Him who gives me strength."

Plantation Life

Down South where I grew up there were only two ways for black men to make money: farming and more farming. Most of the black families that lived on the plantations had to work in the cotton fields, except for those who were fortunate enough to live in the overseer's house or those who had the job of taking care of his family.

The plantation owners let us live in a house which had been built at the owner's expense. In exchange, we worked their fields. They usually paid all of the black folks $2.50 for picking one hundred pounds of cotton. We worked five and a half days a week on the plantations.

Everybody on the plantations got Saturday afternoon off to take care of their personal business. For example, we could browse around, set on the stoop, eat ice cream, and play in the little yard behind the general store. Sometimes we were even allowed to go into the store to pick out a few groceries that we might need during the next week.

If the owner of the store was in a good mood, he might even give us some change back when we paid him for the items we bought with all of our wages. However, it didn't seem to matter what we needed or what we wanted to buy because we were allowed to buy only the same kinds of items we had bought the week before, anyhow. Everybody knew we were being cheated, but we didn't dare say anything, Even if we did say something, it wouldn't do any good! "Help! Doesn't anybody hear my cry?" I wondered so often.

Even now, in 1998, I truly believe that many blacks are still too cautious to speak out when it comes to many different issues which come up because they are afraid that they will be misunderstood if they do make their thoughts known.

Therefore, they keep quiet.

On the other hand, many whites are glad that they do keep still on these issues because, when they do, the whites still feel as if they still "have their thumb on them and they have control over them," even though slavery ended over one hundred years ago. It's for that reason, because slavery ended so long ago, that I believe it's time that more white folks woke up and realized that some of the black people in our nation are unique and intelligent, too. I mean, gee whiz, look how much black people have progressed with hardly any education. Think how much black people could advance if education had been equal to that of the white folks! As a black individual the thought at times makes one bitter, even more so if you have not allowed God to free you.

To get back to my story.... When I was about nine years old I didn't realize that the Lord had said that we were to commit ourselves "to one another" (Ephesians 5:21, NIV) and that He would "rescue me from every evil attack and bring me safely to His heavenly kingdom..." (II Timothy 4:18 NIV). Boy, I wish that I had known it then as well as I know it now! Why? I suppose it was because all of the situations that He allowed me to endure made me stop and realize that there's nothing that God cannot do, but He is in control of all things if, and only if, I take my hands off of the controls!

Anyhow, the only kind of farming that a black man could do at that time was to work on the plantation for about seven or eight years until he "proved himself." Then, maybe, just maybe, the owners might let him rent the land and he might come to be what they called a sharecropper. After he became a sharecropper, he would be able to farm the land like he always had, but he would then get a portion of the crops. His family's future would depend entirely on his farming ability and how well he took care of the land. The plantation owners would give him about six acres to nourish and to plant with cotton, corn, and other crops. It would depend upon how hard he worked and the quality of his yearly harvests as to whether or not he would eventually own the land because after all was said and done, it was mainly because the owner had to get his share of the harvest first which sometimes turned out to be quite a lot. Usually, the best portion went to the owner even though the farmer and his family had done all of the work to produce the harvest.

After seven or eight more years the sharecropper might then be able to finally become the owner of the land. By that time, of course, he was usually a very old man. If he had children they had to pick up where he left off, working the land, and maybe owning it eventually. If the farmer or his children (if he had died while farming the land), weren't able to "prove themselves," by farming the land properly or if they couldn't "make a go of it" in their given allotment of time they as well as their families would have to continue to be just hired hands on "someone else's farm" as long as they stayed there. The ramifications of these circumstances were that he or his children may never get a chance to become sharecroppers if the owners didn't think the harvests were good enough. If that were the case, they may never be able to rent or come to own the land that they and their families had "worked" as long as they had lived on that farm. It was always a judgment call on the part of the owner because most of the owners liked the cheap labor which the black people provided under those circumstances, so it took longer to become a land owner than it may have taken if an impartial person had made the decision.

For example, I want to take a second to talk about my Grandfather Buster as a sharecropper. He had been a hired hand on Mrs. Francis Kate's farm, but over the years he proved his farming abilities and became a sharecropper. He and his family had worked very hard to bring in good harvests for many years. They were such good sharecroppers that they helped Mrs. Kate become a very wealthy woman. I guess she must have realized how much hard work my grandfather's family had done because, before she died, she promised my Grandfather Buster that his family would never suffer for anything if he and his children would just promise to stay on her farm and work it. My grandfather kept his promise in as many ways as he could control. However, he couldn't keep the promise completely because he couldn't keep the parts of the promise which involved some of his children because some of them left and went in various directions. When they got older some of them moved to other plantations. After getting married, because of their circumstances, others did not work on the farm at all anymore. Some of those children went north whereas others went south to Florida. Almost all of his children left that area in Georgia.

Everyone except my Uncle Josh with his family and my Aunt Marie with her Family left Mrs. Kate's farm. Those two families decided to stay on her farm and to work the land of her "plantation."

Sometime around 1987 as Mrs. Kate grew older and more feeble, she didn't know quite what to do with her 350 acres near Midville, Georgia, where I was born and had lived for a while with my grandparents and my parents, so, to my Uncle Josh's surprise, she willed that whole plot of land to him and to his entire extended family; all of his children and grandchildren.

I truly believe that God had been at work in her heart while she was sick because, before that time, she had been a very mean racist woman who would apply the whip to someone without hesitation. I had even witnessed her cruelty myself.

I'll never forget one particular day when she drove up into our yard and my mother asked her for some food. I watched as a little red-haired angry woman came out to the car, swearing, and she refused to give us any food because my mother hadn't worked for about a week. You see, she had been sick and I couldn't take her place because I had had to stay home to take care of her as well as my sisters and brothers for the entire week, so she said "we didn't earn our board that week."

We were living on her other plantation called "Steebottom" near Waynesboro, Georgia, at the time. Only God knows what happened to that plot of land after she died. It was more than 350 acres, but I don't know who worked it or bought it.

However, because of God's work in her heart, she had become a completely changed person. She really changed a lot before she was laid to rest, and for that I give the glory to God. I prayed since then that she repented of all of her wicked deeds before she died.

Now, back to my own immediate family. Our family moved around a lot from one plantation to another. For instance, as you read above, I was born on the Francis Kate Place Plantation, but my family moved to the E. L. Scott Plantation when I was about ten years old and we stayed there until I was about fifteen years old. Then everyone except my father moved back to the Francis Kate Place Plantation for a while. After that, my mother moved to Mr. Scott's nephew's place and to various other places before she moved to Elmira, New York.

I can remember one year in particular during the time that my father was a sharecropper on the E. L. Scott Plantation. He had had a very good year and he had made $800 by selling his portion of the vegetables in town. One day, he borrowed Mr. Scott's truck and drove us to my Grandmother Della's house about thirty miles away. While my mother and the rest of the family were visiting with my grandparents, my father decided to go out with some of his "friends" to drink some corn liquor. On the way home he was so drunk that he ran the truck into a tree. No one was hurt, but the truck had a slight dent in it.

I remember it so well because Mr. Scott threatened to kill my father over that incident. However, instead, he went down to the bank which held my father's account and withdrew all of my father's money, EVERY LAST CENT Of it! Without saying anything to anyone, asking my father for the money or anything else, he just TOOK all of it. There was no question about where it went, either. You see, white folks were able to do that, and many things worse than that to black folks down

South at that time. I wondered to myself, "If my father had not had the money, would Mr. Scott have killed him?" I guess I'll never know the answer to that question.

A very inhumane overseer whom I once called "Old Man Crockett" worked on the E.L. Scott Plantation. He was about the most ruthless white man that I had ever met except that one who tried to rape me. He HATED black people and he did not hesitate to prove it. It was because of him that I began to really <u>hate</u> white people. Today, I believe that it was only by the grace of God that I do not still feel that way because at that time I had every reason to hate white folks deep in my heart. Why? Well, all of those white people in my childhood seemed to be so evil! I probably would have hated all whites if it hadn't been for my godly Grandmother Della who taught her children and all of her grandchildren, including me, that, no matter what white people do to us, God is "faithful and He will strengthen and protect (us) from the evil one." (11 Thessalongians 3:3 NIV) That means that He will see us through all sorts of trials and troubles, no matter what they are. I just praise God every day that, over the years, He has drawn me ever closer to Himself and that He has helped me to love all of those who have abused me: people like Arthur Crockett, E. L Scott, Nurse Green, "the doctor in the blue suit," Mrs. Francis Kate, the list goes on...

One reason that I hated "Old Man Crockett" was because he would come galloping through the cotton fields, frill speed ahead, using his big, overbearing brown horse to make "sport" of chasing and trying to run down our little black boys. Another reason was that he would whip the boys across their backs if he caught them taking a break. As far as I am concerned, one of the worst things this animal of a man did, though, was that he took the older black girls out into the woods, forced them to do some very evil things, and raped some of them. We were often quietly crying, "Help! Help! Help! Doesn't ANYBODY hear our cries for help?"

We all knew this was going on, but we also felt very helpless when it came to doing anything about it. We all hated him for what he did! I really did not yet know down deep in my heart that "the Lord (would really) rescue me from every evil attack,", that He would "bring me safely to His heavenly kingdom" (11 Timothy 4:18a, NIV); and that He is always "faithful" in doing so. (II Thessalonians 3:3, NIV) Oh, how I really wish I had known that then!

[Most white plantation owners always felt superior to all black people. They would use the black women who would eventually become pregnant. Most of the time they would ship the baby to a different plantation so no one would know who fathered the child. That's the way the black race and the white race became so racially mixed that we now have many high yellow or mulatto people who can pass for *whites," others who are light brown, and still others who look like "blacks." Sometimes the plantation owners or people in high society would bribe the midwives to cause the child to be born dead to avoid further problems," The underhanded things which were done by the people in high society in the South were extremely unbearable. I find them almost too unbearable to think about even at the time of this writing. However, from what I hear, much of this has not changed in the deep South even at this time,]

Another reason that I think I must have had more hate in my heart for "Old Man Crockett" than ANYONE else in the world was because he was the man who ultimately drove my father away from home. I remember that incident just as plainly in my mind as if it had happened yesterday. I was fifteen and pregnant with my first child I had a deep craving for fish, so my father went down to one of the closest fishing holes one bright sunny day to catch some fish for me. I can truly say that that's one thing for which I loved my father. He would risk anything within reason to make his beloved family members happy.

When my father didn't come home that day, and for a long period of time afterward, I believed that he had been run out of town just because he had taken time off work to go fishing for me. It made me feel so guilty! I cried often when no one was looking. However, I found out later that what had actually happened was that "Old Man Crockett" was after my father "because of a woman."

According to my source, there was a young high yellow woman who was black, but who looked white, whose name was Caldonia who worked down at the little local store. I don't really know whether my father was interested in her or not. All I really know is that she used to smile at my father whenever he went into the store. Mr. Crockett didn't like her smiling at my father at all because Caldonia was his black mistresses. He was so jealous that he sought to kill my father. Although I didn't think that Mr. Crockett loved that woman enough to kill for her, it was the "principle of the thing" as far as he was concerned. The idea of a black man trying to take something that belonged to a white man just didn't settle too well in the South at that time and it still doesn't. My father had been chased away, My family had been separated! Again, I cried, "Doesn't anybody care? Help! Doesn't anybody hear my cry?"

"Old Man Crockett" was a very wicked man! He came down to the fields looking for my father the day that my father went fishing. Carrying a shot gun, he looked everywhere that my father could possibly hide and talked to everyone who might tell him where my father was at the time. I was so scared! I didn't know it, but somehow my mother had gotten word to Mr. Robert Davis, a friend of the family, and had asked him to get word to my father as soon as possible wherever he was fishing. She also asked Mr. Davis to tell my father not to come back home because "they were gunnin' for him Mr. Davis was so nice that he took my father to

Augusta, Georgia, to my Uncle Lindsey's house. Uncle Lindsey then gave my father, who was frightened for his life, enough money for a bus ticket to get to my Aunt Ruth's house in Newark, New Jersey, My father stayed with her until 1959. During his stay there, he discovered that the rest of the family had migrated to Elmira, New York, so he decided to try to join us.

When I close my eyes I can still visualize the scene as the drama unfolded at the time that my father disappeared. It was almost dusk, and there was a golden sunset through which there were streaks of red orange light along with some pinkish orange streaks. I can still see those restless black horses standing, snorting occasionally, in the front yard while their riders were holding flashlights, shining them through the windows of our tiny run-down unpainted shack. I guess they thought my father may have been in the house somewhere. Five of the white men who had come on horseback to gun down my father were looking around the yard. This happened in 1953, a couple of months before my first son Johnny was born. I wondered again, "Doesn't ANYBODY care what happens. Doesn't ANYBODY hear my pleas for help? Does ANYBODY hear my cry?"

After talking with my mother later, I discovered that she knew what would happen if he had come back to the plantation on that fateful day. We had all seen similar things happen to other families before, but I didn't think it would ever happen to my family, so I hadn't paid much attention to the emotions involved between the family members when it happened to others. I didn't get emotionally involved with other families because we had seen the overseer go after any "black folks" who tried to do something nice for these other black families with a shot gun whenever he found out that they were involved in any way. Did ANYBODY hear their cries?

A couple of months after Johnny was born, they came back again, still looking for my father. We might as well have been "slaves" for the way we were sometimes treated. They were very persistent! However, by the time they came back the second time, my father had been living with my Aunt Ruth in Newark, New Jersey, for four months or more, but I didn't know that at the time.

None of our immediate family were certain of the location of my father. So, even though my father was gone, my mother and the rest of us were all frightened half out of our wits. I can still see my mother hiding under the bed with all of us (children) as we trembled with fear that the white men were going to kill us. Quietly, while we were so afraid and huddled under the bed, I uttered another cry in desperation, "HELP!! We need help! Doesn't anybody hear my cry?

Doesn't ANYBODY care?"

That was the day, as I shivered in fright under that bed that I swore before the Lord that I was going to kill "Old Man Crockett" for what he had done to my father and to our family. Of course, I never told anybody how I felt at the time because it was a secret between me and God.

White people kill blacks even today just as the overseer tried to kill my father then.

For instance, eighteen years ago (New Year's Day, 1980), someone who was related to the E. L. Scott family shot and killed my father somewhere near the E. L. Scott General Store. He was shot in the head and dragged to his own front porch of the little two room, run-down shack in which he was living at the time across the highway from the store. They left him there to bleed to death to be found by someone else. As far as I know, my father's murderer is still running around loose today.

The darkest and hardest day of my life that I had to work through with the help of my Lord was when I had to go back down South to pick out a coffin, and make funeral arrangements for my father.

My brothers and sisters, even though they were all grown and some were married at the time, experienced a dreadful time. It seemed like there was nothing I could do to help or any way I could even console them on that sorrowful day. That's when I realized I couldn't continue to hold anything against Pat because, when I saw her tears as she looked at my father at the funeral home, my heart was sad and heavy for her, too. I went over and gave her a loving hug, told her that I loved her, and that everything would be all right. I suddenly realized that she was part of my family, the amazing thing is that she looks like me, too.

Just as an explanation to identify Pat: After my father and mother decided to "try again" in Elmira, they moved my brothers and sisters who had been living with me until then into their new apartment on John Street.

After a period of time my father started cheating on my mother again and decided to return to the Deep South where he rented a house across the highway from the E. L. Scott General Store. About that time he took up with a woman by the name of Mae Lee and they had a little girl whom they named Willie Lee, but whom we nicknamed "Pat."

Even though I knew that none of my father's doings was Pat's fault, I was very hurt and I couldn't understand at the time that I found out about her why she had to be part of my father's life. I was only nineteen at the time and I also felt jealous and cheated of my father's love.

It had hurt me very deeply when he decided to move back down South because I felt in my heart that I might not ever see him alive again and my fears came true, I didn't! I felt horrible the day he left. I still wondered if the Lord was hearing my cries for help. I cried for many days.

I still have nightmares about my father being killed, especially since there was no one in the family down South to help him, these nightmares have stayed with me because I believe his murderer is still running loose somewhere and there is nothing I can do about it!

As I think back, it is only by the grace of God that I have been able to maintain my sanity. You see, I know that someday God will put an end to the murder, sin, and abuse which goes on around me, especially that which comes back to my mind every time I return to the deep South for one reason or another.

It wasn't until many years after the time when "Old Man Crockett" came gunning for my father, while I was visiting my family in Waynesboro, that I heard that Mr. Crockett had died. The person who told me about it didn't say very many nice things about him, either. However, she did say that he had suffered a lot before he died. I didn't feel too sad about his death because of the anger, the resentment, the hate, or maybe the rage which I had buried so deeply within myself for so many years. But in spite of everything, I really felt bad in my heart to know that he had suffered before he died. Do you wonder, "Why?" Well, even though he had been so ruthless and mean to me and my family when I was young, I had come to know that God loved him, too. Since my childhood, I have asked God to forgive me for the way I had felt about Mr. Crockett over the years.

How can I forgive him and feel this way? It is not because he is dead, but because I am a changed person! I accepted the Lord, Jesus Christ, as my Savior when I was about 16 years old after I had moved back to the Francis Kate Place Plantation. I was first baptized at that time. I have truly thanked God many times that

He came into my heart and that I truly know Him as my Lord and my Savior.

I felt so sad, though, that Mr. Crockett might not have known the Lord before his death. I believe that, perhaps, some of the suffering that God allowed him to go through before his death may have been some of the punishment that he may have received for the evil deeds that he did to us. Perhaps, though, God may have allowed him to go through the suffering just so he might look up to Him, that he might see Him as his Lord — as his only Help in his last hours, and ultimately, to ask Him for the salvation of his soul, After all, Jesus Christ died for all of us while we were still sinners and our only way to heaven is to accept Him as our Savior (Ephesians 2:8-9; NIV).

I have had to work through all of my feelings which 1 have had toward Mr. Crockett. The healing process, including the courage to unmask my anger for him, has taken a long time. I have had to bring it before God, and put it squarely on the shoulders of Christ many times where it really belongs. Sometimes I have found myself trying to pick this burden up again, but Jesus said we are to cast all of our cares upon Him, so again I lay my burden at His feet. This healing process has meant my forgiving everybody involved in this hurtful situation. It has also meant my surrendering my desire for a vindictive triumph over Mr. Crockett. I had to allow God's forgiving love to wash my guilt-plagued soul as white as snow (reference, Psalms 51: 7, NIV). The healing power of God is GREAT! Praise the Lord! I thank God for His GRACE every day, as I remember our instructions in Matthew 6:12 (NIV) where Christ teaches us to pray, "Forgive us our debts as we also have forgiven our debtors." That means that, if I want God to pardon all of my wrongdoings after my salvation, I must forgive others for everything they have done wrong against me.

It also says, in Ephesians 4:31, 32 (NIV) that we should "get rid of all bitterness, rage and anger, brawling and slander, along with every form of malice. Be kind and compassionate to one another, forgiving each other, just as in Christ God forgave (us)."

Then, in Colossians 3:12,13 (NIV), we are told ...as God's chosen people, holy and dearly loved," that we are to clothe ourselves "with compassion, kindness, humility, gentleness and patience." We are also told to "bear with each other and forgive whatever grievances (we) may have against one another. Forgive as the Lord forgave (us)." The Scriptures continue in the next verse, Colossians 3:14 (NIV), telling us "...over all these virtues put on love, which binds (us) all together in perfect unity." It has been a long difficult process, but His grace is truly sufficient for me now that I have learned to "let go" and to "let God" handle the whole situation.

My Trip to the Hospital

When I was about twelve years old, I guess I must have just worked myself into a tizzy and my poor body had just had enough! I was completely exhausted, but I didn't dare tell my mother. Since I couldn't tell my mother how tired I was, my body spoke out plainly for me. All I can remember is my falling off the front steps of our run-down unpainted shack on the E. L. Scott Plantation. Oh, did that hurt! It hurt so much that I was not able to move. I couldn't move any part of my body, it felt like my body was completely broken apart.

Of course my mother was out in the warm sunny weather picking cotton. It wasn't until she came home about noon that she found me lying on the ground. 1 was almost unconscious. The only thing that I could really hear was my mother yelling for my father. My father came running to our house from where he was working in the cotton field. As soon as he arrived, my father picked me up and put me in my bed which was a hay mattress in the house. While my mother stayed with me, my father ran to the overseers' house for help. He cried out, "Please help my little girl! She needs a doctor! She is very, very sick!" Before he ever reached their house my father and the overseer rushed to get Doctor Green in town which was a twenty mile trip. He was an older doctor and he was very kind. The only thing that I remember him telling my mother and father was that I needed medical attention at the nearest hospital which was fifty miles from where we were living at the time. The only way they could transport me to the hospital was by using the black hearse which the undertaker used to transport dead people to the cemetery during a funeral. I'll never forget that dark and dreary evening in October, 1950. I was so sick that I didn't quite know what was going on, but I remember thinking that I must be very close to death if they were using a hearse. The doctor told my mother and my father that I had the flu and meningitis.

Because my condition was so serious, I was taken to the hospital in Augusta, Georgia, where I received much better care. We waited many hours to see the next doctor! I was so weak that I could just barely stand up, but the doctors and the nurses at the hospital must not have realized how sick I actually was because it seemed like they checked me in just to get me out of the way! Again, I wondered, "Does anybody know I'm here? Why have I just been 'put aside' while everyone else was being helped? Why are they ignoring me when I am so sick? <u>Doesn't anybody care about ME</u>?"

After a long, long time, I was finally put in another room, a very dark room, at which time they closed the shades and the doctor left the room. I had to wait there for what seemed like hours, hours, and more hours. By the time they finally came back in to see me, I had almost reached the state of unconsciousness. Just before I passed out the doctor told my mother and my father that I would probably not live through the night, I can barely remember hearing my mother let out a loud yell, "Oh, my God, have mercy!" At that point I was so depressed that I almost hoped for death because I felt so hopeless and helpless.

However, I know now that God had other plans for me. I didn't know it then, but He had heard my cries for help because I prayed to the Lord that I would get better and that I would be able to go home again. I believe, now, that I accepted the Lord as my Savior at the age of twelve, but I really didn't realize it at the time. You see, I always remember hearing my grandmother and grandfather, as well as my mother, say to me, "Call on the Lord and He will hear you." The reason that I really think that I asked Jesus to be my Lord and Savior at that time, even though I didn't fully realize it, is because I began feeling better about many things.

PRAISE THE LORD!

The Doctor and Nurse Hall came in while I was closed up in that dark room at which time he gave me a shot. I must have passed out or fallen asleep while I was praying because the sun was shining, the birds were singing, and I could hear the hustle and bustle of breakfast trays and other morning sounds when I opened my eyes. They then moved me to a regular room.

It was at that point that I got more acquainted with Nurse Hall, one of the nicest people I had ever met up until then. One of the things I remember best is that Nurse Hall was the first person to come into my room that morning. She was smiling and she cheerfully said, "How are you this morning' Darlin'? Your parents are waiting outside to come in to see you."

My mother and my father came in. As my mother looked down at the bed, she cried, "Thank God, you're feeling better."

My father held me in his arms and, in his own words, he said, "You're goin' to be all right Coota Gal." (Coota Gal was the nickname my father had given me when I was a wee little girl.)

He sat on my bed holding me in his arms, he said, "Look, Coota Gal, baby, yo' mother an' I are goin' to leave soon to go home and see about the res' of the kids."

You see, one of the neighbor ladies was taking care of the rest of my sisters and brothers while my mother and father were away from home awaiting news from the doctor about my condition. When my father said he was leaving. I didn't want to be left there alone in this big strange building, so I cried so hard that I couldn't stop.

Nurse Hall came in to see what in the world was the matter with me! She wanted to know why I was so upset. When she found out, she gently said, "Don't cry, honey, I will give you some ice cream, but you have to promise me that you'll stop crying. You'll have to dry your eyes first." She said this with such melody and love in her voice that I knew that she really cared for me. She had expressed love for me! Oh, I loved her so much for that! I believe, that she must have been one of God's angels who had been put here on earth. After I dried my eyes, she left. When she came back, she was carrying a nice little dish of scrumptious vanilla ice cream.

My mother and father stayed in my room with me until she got back with the ice cream, but as soon as she got back, they left. My father promised that one of them, either my mother or my father, would come to see me every day after work. (They would like to have come to see me more often, but they were fifty miles away from the hospital and they couldn't just take time off from work whenever they wanted because they were on the plantation. For any family member to take time off during working hours, I had to be either near death or dead.) When I look back, I praise God, because they kept their promise! One of them was there every single day, rain or shine, until the day I was discharged from the hospital.

I want to pause for a minute and give you a little update on my stay in the hospital. While I was there, my depression got so bad that I used to dread to see the mornings come because that was the time of the day that the nurse would come to take me downstairs to have the doctor draw fluid off of my spine! Oh, I was in so much pain and that needle that he used seemed so big that I thought they were really trying to kill me! Every time they brought me back to my room, I used to stand in front of a great big picture window and look out over the big city of Augusta. I wondered if there was anybody out there who really understood what I was going through, or who really heard my cries for help as well as my cries of pain.

As I stood there, I felt so alone. Why? I believe that it was because I really didn't understand what was happening to me at the tender age of twelve. However, as I gazed out the window I remembered that Grandmother Della used to sing a song that went something like this:

"Must Jesus bear the cross alone, And all the world go free? No, there's a cross for everyone, And there's a cross for me."

As I meditated upon those words, they always brought a peace to my soul while I was in the hospital.

I had to stay in the hospital for about two whole months. so it was after Christmas when they finally discharged me. The doctors, nurses, and the other people at the hospital were very nice to me at Christmas time. They gave me candy, oranges, a doll, and a beautiful dainty china tea set as Christmas presents.

"Good morning, darlin' or 'Good evening, little one, how do you feel today?" as she did while I was in her care. She had such a nice influence on me that I call my grandchildren "little ones". It is so ironic. One of my granddaughters also reminds me a lot of Nurse Hall.

To get back to my story about Nurse Green, I will never forget that "big, fat red lady"! She was a black woman, but she was very "red" and she was just as mean as her "redness" made her look! As I remember, she wore some kind of yellow "nurse's outfit", and that didn't make my perception of her any better at all!

Nurse Hall had been so different from Nurse Green! Nurse Hall had smiled just like an angel every day. She made me feel so "warm" and "fuzzy" inside! Oh, how I liked that feeling because for the first time in my life she made me feel "good" and "loved"(as I was) instead of for what I could do for someone! To this day I deeply believe that she was an angel sent from God. God knew <u>exactly</u> what I needed as a child, especially after my experience of being so sick and having lived on that dreadful plantation with "Old Man Crockett"! Nurse Hall's simple gestures of kindness gave me hope that I could meet kind people, even if only for a short period of time and even though many years would pass before meeting someone as kind as her again. Thoughts of her often made me smile!

Even though my mother and my father came to visit me every day, I was still lonely and scared — mostly, just plain scared! I was so afraid that something was going to happen to me. Why? Well, I believe it was because, at that time, it was very difficult for black families who lived on the plantation to get to see the doctor when a member of the family became ill. When most of the black kids whom I had known on the plantation got sick, nothing would be done about it. However, I was in a hospital a long way from the plantation where I didn't really know anyone, with all sorts of tests being done on me with no explanation of what was being done or why, so I had all kinds of crazy thoughts.

But, as I look back on that time in my life, I was one of those who had been blessed by God, even though I didn't know it at the time because I hadn't truly accepted Jesus as my Savior yet. My Grandmother Della's prayers probably had a lot to do with my living through this ordeal. Why do I say this? Because, as I have noted before, God had a plan for my life, even though I knew nothing about "His will" at that particular time or the power of prayer.

For instance, I did not realize that God could be my refuge and my strength, and "...an ever-present help in trouble." (Psalm 46:1, KJV). Nor did I know that the "Fear of man will prove to be a snare, but whoever trusts in the Lord is kept safe...." (Proverbs 29:25, KJV) because at that time I didn't really trust <u>anyone</u> whom I could put my arms around, so I could NOT trust or love someone whom I couldn't see or hear — such as God.

As I lay on my hospital bed, scared and lonely, I remember one day when a different doctor came into my room to draw some blood from my finger. He was wearing a BLUE suit. I was crying a lot because I didn't want him to take any of my blood. He called me a "black nigger**" and he said, "Damn your specimen!"

I had no idea what he was talking about when he said, "specimen," and I didn't ask anyone what he meant, so I dreaded being left in the dark after he talked to me in that manner. In my immature mind, I thought that he might come back to kill me, or to do something horrible to me. I also thought, "Maybe he was disappointed that I hadn't died!" I had a very hard time trying to sleep after my encounter with him. Does Anybody Hear My Cry?

Every time he came into my room and pricked my finger to take some blood, I looked at his face. It seemed to me that he had "an evil look in his eye." Frightened, and scared beyond description, I just stared at him as he drew and held up my blood samples to examine them to see if he would need to draw some more blood" After seeing the anger in his face I lost all of my trust in him. I had always had respect for doctors before my encounter with "the doctor in the blue suit," but I lost all of the respect I had ever had after his treatment of me. His horrible "bedside manner" made me feel even worse rather than better, it took longer for me to get well enough to go home.

In spite of the way he treated me every day, I eventually became stronger and stronger.

Then, as time passed, one day it was time for me to leave the hospital. But, by that time I really didn't <u>want</u> to leave the hospital. I was surprised that I felt that way, but, as I think back, I really shouldn't have been surprised that I reacted in that manner. You see, in the hospital I was protected from the overseer and I didn't have to work on the plantation every day. I could be a "child" for a change and I could enjoy life like all of the other children.

When my day of departure came, even though I didn't want to leave, I slowly packed the few little things that I had brought to the hospital and the presents which they had given me for Christmas. I packed my beautiful little tea set with extreme care — more carefully than I packed anything else. It was so pretty — so delicate and precious — that I wanted to make sure that I didn't break it as I packed it for the long trip to the plantation. It was the most precious gift I had ever been given and I wanted it to last forever!

I had tears in my eyes as I prepared to leave because my favorite nurse, Nurse Hall, had not come to see me, so I figured that she was not going to be able to say, "Good-bye". As they were wheeling me down the hall, as I left the hospital, I kept looking around, trying to find her smiling face, but I couldn't see her anywhere.

When I finally dried my tears I was surprised to see my father who had come to pick me up and take me home from the hospital riding with a man by the name of Mr. Jake Dukes. They had borrowed an old greyish pickup truck from the plantation with which to take me home. Of course, as usual, Mr. Dukes was drunk from drinking corn liquor.

Yes, you guessed it! My precious little tea set! About halfway home from the hospital Mr. Dukes hit something in the middle of the road. He was so drunk and driving so fast my beautiful precious little tea set went flying out of my arms and was broken into a million pieces or, so it seemed. Of course, I cried all of the rest of the way home. I tried to piece the tea set back together after I got home, but I couldn't because there were just too many dishes that had been broken into too many pieces. I couldn't tell which piece went where. So, I kept the rest of the set, and the pieces of the broken dishes, in an old shoe box until my mother made me throw it out one dark, rainy day. Again, I wondered why I couldn't ever have anything nice because all of the rest of my presents had been ruined by my little brothers and sisters, and, now I had to dispose of the most precious gift I had been given, again I cried from within, "Doesn't anybody hear my cry? Doesn't anybody care about ME??

I was very upset with Mr. Dukes — mainly because he NEVER said that he was sorry about the accident causing my beautiful tea set to be broken. Instead, he had just <u>grinned</u> when the accident happened. He was so drunk that he thought it was funny, I guess. In this day and age, he would have been thrown in jail for "DWI". When I look back, oh, how I wish that they had laws like that in those days.

However, I eventually did forgive him after I was saved.

Several weeks after I arrived at my home on the plantation from the hospital, my work schedule resumed and I began to work in the cotton field again. You see, I had no choice about when I was to return to working the fields because, one day when I was sitting out on the porch enjoying the sunshine and trying to get my strength back, "Old Man Arthur Crockett" came by the house and wanted to know why I wasn't out in the field. I said, "My mother left me home until I get my strength back." I was really feeling much better, but I was not really feeling good enough to go out in the field to pick his cotton.

Before he left me that day, he said, "Don't let me come here tomorrow and find you sitting here and not in the field. I'm not going to have "niggas" sitting around not doing anything! Tell your daddy and your mamma that I'll be back tomorrow and you tell them that I want you in that field, working!"

I wondered, again, "Doesn't ANYBODY hear my cry? Here, I, am, just out of the hospital and Old Man Crockett wants me to work in the fields! HELP!! ISN'T THERE ANYBODY OUT THERE! I DON'T WANT TO GO TO WORK TOMORROW! Does ANYBODY out there hear me? Since I couldn't get an answer from anybody human in times like this, I had two "unseen friends" to whom I called.

Here I was and "something bad" had happened to me again, so I called upon my two "unseen friends" and talked to them about my problems. I named one of my "unseen friends" "Berta Mae" and the other, "John Abbott". My cry to them was, "Oh, John Abbott! Oh,

Berta Mae! Please help me I feel so sad in my heart!" I didn't know it then, but I believe that I was on the brink of a "nervous breakdown" without God's influence in my life because I would cry continuously to those "unseen friends" until I felt as though they were right by my side.

Talking about my "unseen friends", as I think back, I believe that I thought, at that time, that I was trying to reach out to my parents because I really couldn't talk to them like I wanted to be able to talk. Therefore, I would call on my two "unseen friends." I carried these two "unseen friends" with me through my early adult life, too. However, when I began studying the Bible and, later in life I started learning about angels, I began thinking that "John Abbott" and 'Berta Mae may have been angels sent by God to help me because I then realized that angels DO have names, just like the Angel Gabriel.

Getting back to my story, I cried myself to sleep that night, thinking about how I had to go out to work in the field the next day. You see, I felt that maybe I wasn't strong enough to go back to work in the cotton fields yet. Even though I had started working in the fields much earlier in my life, it was still VERY HARD WORK for me at the age of twelve.

I gradually regained my strength after my harrowing trip to the hospital. After being home for about a month, I was again working "full blast," baby-sitting my sisters and brothers again, doing all kinds of farm work and working in the cotton fields. Before my trip to the hospital, I had helped my father saw down trees, trim off the branches, and chop wood for the fire as well as cooking. It seemed like we worked nonstop. Boy, was that HARD WORK!

Now, I was right back at it, again working just as hard as ever. This went on until I was seventeen years old in 1955.

I would have to get up early every morning. I helped my father feed the chickens and the rest of the animals about five o'clock. I could always tell when five o'clock arrived because our rooster, "Red," would always crow at that time and he wouldn't quiet down until my father went out to feed him. Boy, did I HATE to hear that rooster at that time of the day! That meant that I had to get up and begin working hard again. We would finally finish feeding all of the animals about six o'clock in the morning.

When we finished, my mother would always pray with us before we ate our breakfast of "a biscuit, corn mush, and fatback". I really didn't want to go to work, but I reluctantly went out to the big hot, dusty field of cotton around seven o'clock with my father. If my folks were working in fields nearby my mother stayed at the house until about eight o'clock to make sure that the rest of the children in the family were fed and would be all right until I was able to get back to the house. At that point, she would come out to the field and send me back home to baby-sit until around noon when she would come back to the shack to make us some collard greens, corn bread, and roasted sweet potatoes. That was our lunch. Then, between 1:30 and two o'clock in the afternoon, my father and mother went back to the field to pick cotton until about four o'clock. About four o'clock she would come back out to the house and take my place for a while longer. She would then fix a supper of homemade buttermilk biscuits, black-eyed peas, and fresh okra for the family while I went with my father as he went back out to work in the fields that seemed even hotter and dustier than when I had worked in them in the morning. I would then work at my father's side until dusk.

However, if my parents were working in one of the fields which were five or six miles from home, they would have to fix a lunch for themselves to take to work because there was no way for them to return in the middle of the day to check on how we were doing. By the way, mother would have fixed our lunch the night before she left for the fields afar off. We had just about the same lunch almost every day, and it was our favorite. My folks would have to work from sunup until sundown in those horrible fields while I was left at home to care for my brothers and sisters.

As I look back, I often think about the Twenty-third Psalm and how my God has led me through the valley of the shadow of death so many times and I thank Him that I no longer fear any evil! (See the chapter called "Step by Step.")

After studying some of the promises of Jesus, I don't have to worry about anything here on earth. One promise is in John 14:10 KJV, where it says "Let not your heart be troubled; ye believe in God, believe also in me. (2) In my Father's house are many mansions; if it were not so, I would have told you. I go to prepare a place for you. (3) And if I go and prepare a place for you, I will come again, and receive you unto myself, that where I am, there ye may be also." As I reread those beautiful promises, I realize that this earth is not my home and that I am just passing through.

When I think about the whole story of how the Lord took me to the hospital and brought me back safely, I can give Him all of the glory concerning the miracle that He worked in my life.

OH, HOW I PRAISE HIM!

Bless the Lord, O my soul,

And all that is within me, Bless His Holy Name.

He has done great things,

He has done great things,

He has done great things,

Bless His Holy Name.

When meditate upon this song, I can truly say that He has done GREAT things for me!

How can I NOT serve Him? I must serve Him because He is worthy to be praised! He is my God. He is my Salvation. He is the Lily of the Valley, the Bright and Morning Star,... He is the Head Of my Life..., my Strength and my Redeemer. He supplies all my needs. Praise be to God,

Hallelujah!!

Troubles Troubles and More Troubles

My troubles really began about the time I was almost fifteen. I thought I had troubles before but things got worse! Much worse!

You see, I met a young man by the name of Johnny Lee Mells when I was fourteen years old while I was living on the E. L. Scott Plantation. He would come over to visit me every Saturday night. We would sit and talk until about midnight at which time he would go home. One day stands out very vividly in my mind — even to this day. I remember that I was standing at the ironing board, ironing some clothes for my mom and the rest of the family. Johnny had come over to visit for a little while as usual. Suddenly I noticed that he had come up from behind me, and putting his arm around me. I remember him whispering sweet words in my ear; words which still ring in my head today as he said, "You are the most sweetest young lady I ever met. You are the prettiest young lady that I've ever seen. I don't want to just sit around talking about picking cotton and working in the field all of the time." He then slowly pulled me close to him and he began to rub his hands across my body as he asked, "Do you want me? Do you want me as much as I want you?" He gently pulled up my little short skirt, propped me up against the old fashioned fire place and before I realized what was happening I found myself in a situation which would affect me for the rest of my life because we made love to each other very passionately. I think I became pregnant with my first son Johnny that very night.

I wasn't quite sure at the time what exactly had happened that night, but I did know that I felt something come over me like I had never felt before. I felt such a deep love for Johnny! I did not realize that, later in life, he would hurt me just as deeply as I loved him then. Every Saturday night I looked forward to his visit and he would fulfill all of my desires. He always managed to get sexually involved with me every time he came to see me. He was kind, gentle, loving, and he was the best sweet talker around. He could mesmerize me by just talking charmingly to me.

Months went by. It wasn't long before I found myself feeling sick almost every morning. Guess what! Yes, I was pregnant. I didn't know anything about taking care of myself while being pregnant. All I did know was that I liked the idea of being pregnant, I wanted to be pregnant, and I wanted to have Johnny's baby! However, when I told him that I was going to have his baby, he looked at me as though I had just stabbed him in the heart. He slacked off on his visits to my home so my beautiful, joyful, love filled Saturday visits became dreadful Saturday night nightmares. At that young age I thought we could get married because I loved him so much and, after all, I was carrying HIS baby. However, he had no thoughts about marriage in his mind. He had his thoughts on something entirely different even though I didn't fully realize it. It wasn't long before he stopped coming to my house altogether. If I saw him at all, it was when we met by accident. He dropped me like a hot potato! It still brings tears to my eyes when I think about how he treated us — his unborn baby and me.

Another day that I'll never forget is the day when, as I was walking to my friend Alice's house, he passed me quickly in his car just as if I were some of the dirt which was thrown in my face by his car. When I finally arrived at Alice's house, guess who I found sitting on her porch. Yes, Johnny! I guess he had had a crush on her all along and as soon as he heard that I was pregnant he dropped me for her!

Since I had walked this long way to visit Alice, I continued my walk toward the house. As I stepped up to the porch, I shyly said, "Hi," but everyone ignored my presence. It was as if I weren't there at all. Johnny continued his conversation with my friend and her sister. At that time I retreated back into the middle of the yard and stood by their well because Alice, too, had completely ignored me, was not hospitable, and had refrained from inviting me up on her porch.

As I took in this whole scene, the only thoughts which came to my mind were, "I wonder if anyone would pay attention to me if I jumped in this well. Would anybody miss me? Doesn't anybody hear my cry? Doesn't anybody care about me or my unborn baby?"

I am so glad that I didn't jump, though, because both my baby and I would have lost everything forever. I know the Lord was with me because I heard a still, small voice tell me to leave that place, so I turned and sadly walked ever so slowly down the dirt road from whence I had come. All the way home, I couldn't do anything but cry, sob, cry, and sob some more.

Nobody but God knew how I felt at that dreadful time on that hot August afternoon.

Two months later on October 10, 1953, my first son Johnny was delivered by a midwife at my home which was a little dilapidated shack on the E. L. Scott Plantation on a dark, dreary Saturday night.

When Johnny was about three months old, John came by the house to see what our son looked like. At that time, he held his son on his lap for the first time. I could see that he seemed to care, but wonder now if he felt "trapped" because he was only nineteen years old and he had also had lots of childhood problems with his folks. Of course, that didn't help me any because I had to figure out how to take care of, provide food for, and get health care for my new baby and I didn't know much along those lines at the tender young age of fifteen. My mother couldn't help me much because of all of her own health problems and she also had to try to care for all of my brothers and sisters. There were still periods of time when she couldn't go to the field or go get groceries for herself and her family, so I couldn't depend upon her for help, either. In addition to taking care of Johnny, I often had to take over many of her responsibilities in caring for my brothers and sisters.

As I think about the whole situation, I guess she did the best she could under the circumstances because my father had been driven away from home by that time by "Old Man Crockett." Think about it! My father had been deprived of the privilege of being on the plantation when his first grandson "popped into this world."

As I tearfully think about these memories, I guess Johnny wanted to experience the worldly pleasures and sensations, but he didn't want any of the responsibilities that went with them.

Thinking about my own feelings, the day that my son's father walked out of my life is a day that I can remember well. That whole day seemed so dark and dreadful. He walked right out of my life as if I were a nobody ... as if we didn't know each other ... as if we hadn't had any kind of meaningful relationship at all! "Oh, doesn't anybody hear my cry?" I sobbed again and again.

It seemed like my old troubles were starting all over again. However, this time, they were more serious, and they affected me more severely! For all intents and purposes John Lee Mells had walked out of my life and from that day on, I went from one unhappy experience to another as I slid backwards into what seemed like a bottomless pit of "a living hell." I found myself crying, almost continuously, "<u>Doesn't ANYBODY hear my cry</u>? Anybody at all!? Isn't ANYBODY there?"

I now believe that God allowed all of these things to happen the way they did so that I would learn that God was my helper in times of trouble, After all, look at the various and sundry types of struggles I had to endure and the numerous "deep waters" that I had to cross by the time I was only fifteen. For instance, so MANY times I felt like I was drowning and I felt like my life was like a whole big bunch of "deep rivers" and their tributaries which I had to cross. It seemed like each one was even deeper than the last one and more difficult to cross, — much like the Jordan River which was at flood stage when Joshua was trying to lead the children of Israel to the Promised Land in Joshua 3:15a.

To make a long story short, I was left to raise Johnny the best I could with my limited education and resources. At this point in my life, I can truly say that God in His infinite mercy has led me, and sometimes carried me, every step of the way in this endeavor. I would not have been able to do it without Him and His guidance.

When I was almost sixteen years old, a few years after my father was run out of town, a man named Buddy Benjamin, who lived about one mile down the road from us, began coming over to visit our family. Actually, he came over to see my mother: We had never seen him come to the house until after my father left. I guess my mother became lonely because my father was gone. All I know for sure is that, as far as I was concerned, he wasn't going to take my father's place if I had my way! I didn't care how nice he was to us. My father was still alive, so I wasn't going to let Buddy take over in his place!

Mr. Benjamin, as well as some of the other men who visited my mother, also left his share of scars on our lives. However, a big problem arose when my mother became pregnant by him! She got very sick about the time she reached her seventh month of her pregnancy. She called me and told me to go fetch the midwife. I ran as fast as my legs would carry me in the pouring rain on the muddy roads, through the tall wet grass, through the brush, through the cotton field, for what seemed like more than a mile to get a midwife for my mother.

When we, the midwife and I, finally got back, my mother made me stay in the room to help the midwife. Boy, was I ever <u>scared</u>! I was shaking in my boots! The baby was coming! It was the most horrible sight I had ever witnessed in my entire life! I had never seen a puppy or a kitten born, let alone a human baby! Yes, I had had a baby of my own, but I hadn't seen it from that point of view. I was not prepared for that sight at all! In the end, after all of the trouble we had gone through, the baby was born dead. The midwife wrapped the baby in some soft cloth and placed him in an old shoe box that we had around the house. Then, of all things, my mother told the midwife to give the baby to me and she told me to go bury it! Can you imagine that? The thought was horrible enough by itself, but now it was up to me to bury this baby.

I will never forget that awful, horrible, horrid, gruesome day. My little sister Osie and I cautiously walked to the cemetery with the dead baby in our hands. We felt so heavyhearted, and so scared that we held the brown shoe box way out in front of us, as if it were going to bite, or pop up out of the box, or do something else that would be dreadful! That was by far the worst experience that I had ever had in my life — even worse than seeing the baby come through the birth canal! I had to dig the small hole and bury the box! I don't think Osie understood what was really happening, but I went through a lot of trauma after that day! For a long time afterwards, I had nightmares in which I saw myself digging that "grave"! In the nightmare I dug forever, or so it seemed, and the "grave" just didn't seem to get any bigger. I truly felt like I was digging my own grave in my nightmares. Because of this, I resented my mother for a long time. Why? Because she made ME do that horrible deed. Sometimes I still have nightmares as I write about that horrifying night. As an adult I believe that some adult should have been asked to do it, especially since we were so young and impressionable. Oh, how it hurt to bury that little baby!

It seems like I was always the one who was put in the position of a substitute for her or someone else whenever they didn't want to do the "dirty work" or take the responsibility for various types of jobs which were distasteful. I felt like the scapegoat! There were times when I felt like going back to the cemetery, digging up the box which held the baby, bringing it back to the house, giving it back to my mother, and letting <u>her</u> bury it. It was her responsibility, not mine! "Anyhow, why couldn't Buddy Benjamin bury the baby?" I wondered. After all, it was my mother's or his responsibility. Why she ever exposed me to such a painful experience as that turned out to be, I would never know. Even now, I get nauseated just thinking about it.

I still visualize that scene over and over again, especially in my sleep, even to this day!

Sometimes I have to go the Lord in prayer to keep from thinking about it. However, I must remember that God knew what was best in that situation, so I just have to leave it, too, on Christ's shoulders because it is too much for me to deal with by myself. When I begin thinking about it, I have to remember Romans 8:28 which says that all things work together for those who love God and are called according to His purpose. At other times, I remember Isaiah 26:3 which promises that God will keep me in perfect peace if I keep my mind <u>on Him</u> because I trust Him. After I remember these verses and other promises which He has made, I can go on with the rest of my life.

A friend said that it reminded her of what one of her pastors once said as he illustrated this point in one of his sermons, "Our lives on earth are like a piece of cross-stitch needlework. One day in our lives is like one stitch in the entire picture. It may be a yellow stitch surrounded by four different colors such as pink, red, green, and blue. As the yellow stitch, we have no idea what the whole picture may be by looking at the colors of the stitches which surround us.

However, the Lord can see the whole picture which may be a beautiful bouquet of flowers. Therefore, we must trust Him in everything and completely surrender our lives to His care because He knows what the picture of our lives will look like if we let Him oversee all of the stitch work." That means that he doesn't need our help ... that we shouldn't try to "make the stitches" by taking the needle out of his hand. With His guiding hand the "stitches" of our life will make beautiful completed "work" as we walk through life with our hand in His taking one careful step at a time looking to Him for guidance every day.

There are also times when I think about Philippians 1:6 (KJV) which says that I must be confident that He who has begun "'a good work in you will carry it on to completion until the day of Jesus Christ." Or, perhaps someone reminds me about Psalm 91:4 -7, 10 which tells us that, if we will just trust Him, God will cover us with His wings whenever we ask. Since He is our protector, we need not be afraid of anything at all. If we claim this promise, no evil will happen to us, or to our households! PRAISE GOD!!

My New Life in Elmira, New York

Another unforgettable day for me was the day that my cousins Charley and Louis drove into my mother's dirt yard on the Steebottom Plantation in their shiny black car. The Steebottom Plantation was Francis Kate's place near Waynesboro, Georgia.

It was a very cold day in October, 1955, when Charley asked my mother if he could take me, an eighteen year old teenager, to Elmira, New York, where I could live with him and Aunt May. He thought that I should be able to get a job doing housework for someone. He thought it would help my mother, financially speaking, to take care of my sisters and brothers, However, as I began packing my bag with the few clothes that I had, I was surprised to hear Rosie, my five year old sister who was standing by my side, crying, "Mommy, don't leave me! Mommy, please don't leave me! Mommy, <u>please don't leave me!</u>" Rosie had always called me "Mommy" because it was I who was always taking care of her, not my mother.

When I looked into her sweet little brown eyes and saw her little face with tears streaming down it, I began to cry, too. As I picked up my bags to walk off of the parch to get into the car, she grabbed my leg and was holding onto me tightly, screaming, "Mommy, don't leave me! Mommy, PLEASE don't leave me!" As I approached the car to get into it, she threw her little self on the ground on her knees crying still louder and begging, "Oh, Mommy, PLEASE don't leave me! Mommy, please don't LEAVE me!"

My mother was also crying, saying, "Oh, Rosie, you can't go, too! I can't let you go, too.

I can't let both of my little girls go!"

About that time, I turned to my mother and told her that I couldn't go without Rosie and that I had to take her with me, so I gently picked her up on my way to the car. I couldn't bear to listen to her any longer and I knew I could take care of her. Cousin Charley opened the back door of the car and as we got into the back seat, she squeezed me tightly, saying, "Oh, Mommy. I love you, I love you." Rosie clung to me very tightly all the way to Elmira. If I moved, she moved with me. She wanted to make sure that she was with me when we got to our destination.

As my cousin Charley stepped on the accelerator and drove away from the drab shack which had been my home on that plantation, I can still picture my poor mother standing in the yard, weeping and waving to her two precious daughters as we disappeared from her view.

My New Life in Elmira, New York

We were on our way to a place called Elmira, New York, which was a long, long way from Georgia. Oh, how I was hurting! I was brokenhearted because, not only did I have to leave my mother, but I also had to leave my two year old son Johnny there, too and I did not know if I would ever see him again. I also had to leave my four brothers and my sister Osie in Georgia that day. I was leaving most of my family and all of my friends for some unknown small town which was completely foreign to me in the North.

I wish that my whole family and I had known about God's promise in Psalms 147:3 where it says that God promises to heal broken hearts and bind them up because, if we had, the transition would have been so much easier for me.

However, because I had never heard about it, I cried for many hours as my cousin Charley drove north toward New York State before I was able to settle down just a little. I had mixed feelings about this adventure. On one hand I was happy that I was leaving the plantation in the South, but on the other hand I was extremely sad that I had had to leave most of my family behind because, as I mentioned in the discussion in the chapter about Plantation Life by the time I went to Elmira, my father had left home and had gone to New Jersey.

As we got further down the road and after I got myself a little more composed, I knew that I had to try, somehow, to make things better for my mother and the rest of my sisters and brothers as well as for my two year old son whom I'd had to leave behind.

As we arrived at my cousin Charley's house in Elmira, I remember his wife Willie May coming to the door to greet each of us with a big hug. Everybody addressed her as "Aunt May" because she certainly was like an aunt to everyone.

I had been very anxious during the entire trip as Cousin Charley had driven the long trip north from Georgia because / wondered (a) how Aunt May would accept my sister and me and (b) whether she would like us. Therefore, I was very surprised when she greeted us so warmly with such open arms upon our arrival. She looked into our faces and said, "You poor little darlin's. Come in, come in. Sit down and have somethin' to eat."

I would like to pause a second to tell you a little about my Aunt May. While we were living in her house, she never once made my sister or me feel unwelcome. She was not really my aunt. She was married to one of my second cousins. However, she always made sure that Rosie's and my needs were met just like a loving mother would have done. My sister and I didn't have many clothes when we arrived, but after we had been at Aunt May's house approximately a week, she went out and bought both of us some lovely clothes to wear. You see, my Aunt May was an old-fashioned Baptist Christian. She truly loved us as Christ had loved the world (John 13:34b), paraphrased), She always went to church and made sure that my sister and I went along, too.

My New Life in Elmira, New York

I grew to have such love for my Aunt May that I looked upon her as a mother figure. She was the type of person who, even though I brought lots of trials and tribulations with me when I came from the Deep South, she always took the time to show me what to do to feel better about myself. God was her refuge and strength as His Word teaches in Psalm 46:1 and she knew that the Lord would watch over me when I was overwhelmed because He knew the ministry which He had in store for me. Because the Lord acted through her, she could help me find a little more peace that I had ever had before in my life. Because of the way God used her to help me, I gained more and more peace each time I had a chance to talk to her about any new event which had happened in my life.

It wasn't long before I began working at Dr. Horne's house at 509 Walnut Street in Elmira. My job description included caring for his family, so I eventually felt as though I practically raised his three children. I wasn't making very much money, but I didn't know how to use their many appliances which were all so new to me until Mrs. Horne was able to take the time to teach me how to work them. Oh, how I can remember how my knees shook so often during that first week! I was then in such a completely different environment and I had to learn how to do so many new types of duties. However, I still have to laugh when I think of the first time I saw "Jello" and didn't even know what it was. Also, I was scared to death when she turned the vacuum cleaner on for the first time while I was in the room. I thought I'd never become adjusted to all of the "fancy" new tools with which I would be working with!

After I had been in Elmira for about a month, I was extremely thrilled when I was invited to a birthday party of a second cousin of mine in November — Pastor Johnny L. King. As I think back, I can still see myself in my beautiful green skirt and my nice white blouse which my Aunt May had bought me for that very special occasion. My sister Rosie was wearing her beautiful little new pink, flowered outfit. We both felt so dressed up! When I think of the tattered drab tattered clothes we had worn on the plantation, we were "very dressed up."

I enjoyed myself very much that night because I had never before been to such a breathtaking occasion as a birthday party. However, little did I know how my whole life was about to change completely!

Believe it or not. I met the man whom I would eventually marry at that party Arthur Myers, Sr. There I was, a very timid young lady, feeling so very special as I sat on a nice chair as I took in all that was taking place before my very eyes. I couldn't believe that I had been invited to such a nice party. I didn't want to pinch myself because I was afraid that I was dreaming and would wake up.

I was very surprised when I turned and saw a young man staring at me from across the room as he, too, sat watching what everyone was doing. However, as I paid closer attention to what he was watching, I found that he was spending most of his time gazing at me. My heart began to pound! He eventually walked across the floor and asked me my name. I melted as he looked into my eyes and said, "You are the prettiest girl I've ever seen."

He surprised me even more when he asked my cousin Charley's permission to talk with me. Of course, because I had just come from the Deep South, I was very shy and I didn't know what to say. Finally, however, before I realized what had really happened, I had gathered enough courage to talk to him. He was rather easy to talk with and he was also very friendly. We began to get acquainted as we exchanged information about our differing backgrounds.

Boy, I'm telling you, he was really moving fast. I didn't realize it, but most things seem to happen much more quickly in the Northeast than they do in the Deep South because of the difference in the cultures. Before that night was over, he made me a promise that he would see me "tomorrow" which was a Sunday. Arthur was ten years older than I was and my Aunt May thought he was a little too old for me.

"After all," she reminded me, "you are only seventeen years old." However, on the other hand, my cousin Charley didn't seem to think that Arthur was too old.

There I was! Life in the North was so new, different, and exciting that I very soon found myself dating a man ten years my senior.

On Christmas Eve after we had been dating for only about a month, he surprised me by presenting me with a beautiful, 14-karat gold diamond ring. I was so surprised that my eyes nearly popped out of my head! It was SO BEAUTIFUL! As he slipped it on my finger and asked me to be his wife, I was completely overwhelmed! I felt so excited and so very special — even more special than when my Aunt May bought me the beautiful clothes! I felt like I was in heaven on cloud nine. I had always wanted to get married and to have a beautiful family, so when he asked for my hand in marriage, it was as if my dream had come true. He was like my Prince in Shining Armor!"

After my dark, depressing experience with my son's father in the South, I had finally met the man of my dreams; someone who really wanted to marry me because he loved me. Not only did he want to marry ME — the girl who had worn shoes with curled up toes, but he also wanted to accept my son Johnny as his own, so there we were — engaged to be married. I still couldn't believe it had really happened to me. When I finally pulled myself together, we set a date for February 16, 1956.

To this day, I don't really know why I set the date for the wedding for February 16 except that it was my birthday. I imagine that I did it that way because I was so happy to get married that I just set the date which first popped into my mind and it was also a convenient date. Besides, my birthday seemed just as good as any other day and I would be married on the day which I became eighteen years old, it seemed like a very nice way to celebrate my birthday.

As the days and months rolled by, Arthur and I began to see more and more of each other, growing closer and closer each day. We began going to church together, going to the movies together, and making more plans for the wedding each time we saw each other. We were also making plans for the type of home in which we wanted to live —a house or an apartment, its location, etc.

As I think about Arthur, it makes me think about how eager he was to get married, as well as how sweet and kind he was during our courtship. He treated me with much kindness as well as with respect. I had not been truly "loved" that much by anyone except my grandmother Della up until that time.

I will never forget the day when, as we were reaching the deadlines for the various details of our wedding, we were able to seriously plan out the most minute details of it. By that time, Arthur had moved to Elmira from Savona, New York, so he could get a job at the Arnot Ogden Hospital. I was still working at Dr. Horne's home, making only about thirty-five dollars a week as "bring home pay" for five days' work. I asked myself as well as my Aunt May, "How can I plan my wedding, buy a dress, and purchase all of the necessities for the wedding with such a small amount of money?" At that time she reassured me that everything would work out because she was going to help me all she could by planning the menu and helping me with all of the other necessary things that I needed which included a bridal veil. She was so considerate and loving that she bought me a beautiful white shoulder length veil which I can still visualize today because the cloth was so fine that it reminded me of a fluffy cloud. It had fine lace around the edge of it and flowers on the headpiece.

She and I began planning for the wedding a day or two after Christmas because she kept reminding me that we didn't have much time to get everything done, so I worked very hard and saved up my money to buy my wedding outfit while Arthur was saving to pay for his beautiful blue suit and for the apartment in which we would live after we were married.

As the weeks passed by, we were as busy as little bees, preparing every little detail for that very special day February 16. The menu was made up, the guest list was made out, the invitations were mailed, and a lot of shopping had to be done to find a proper dress and all of the necessities for my wedding. I got a beautiful <u>blue</u> garter belt and I borrowed an old, but pretty, lace handkerchief from my Aunt May.

The only regret that I had about the plans for my wedding was the color of my dress. You see, I really wanted to wear white, but everyone thought, since I had a baby out of wedlock, that it wouldn't be proper for me to get married in white. I was very hurt because I "couldn't wear white," but the Lord was with me as I went shopping and as I walked into the Cameo Shop on North Main Street in Elmira in January, 1956. To my surprise, my eyes fell upon a gorgeous sky blue wedding dress. It was as if God had put that special dress there just for me. (It wasn't until many years later that I discovered that I could have worn white because white represents purity and my marriage itself was pure.]

Little did I know that every time something went "wrong" for me in my mind, that God would show me a better way — His way — to do that which needed to be done. He assured me that it didn't matter about the color of the dress, but what really mattered was that I was getting married! Praise God!

For that reason I bought the beautiful blue satin dress which he had helped me to find and anxiously awaited my very special day — my wedding day.

We got married in Aunt May's and Cousin Charley's beautiful home on High Street which was decorated just special for the occasion. Aunt May must have had to cook for three days because there was enough food at the reception to feed an army. She used her best silverware, her best tablecloths, and she ordered freshly cut floral bouquets from the local florist. I was so surprised to find that she had ordered the most beautiful little blue and white bridal bouquet with flowing satin ribbons! Oh, I was so excited!

However, the night before my wedding, I couldn't get to sleep because I wanted so much for my mother to be there. I knew that she couldn't make it, so I sobbed almost all night. When the next morning came, I rolled out of bed and my sister and I routinely knelt by our bed to pray before beginning the day as we had done every day since we had arrived in Elmira. When I rose from my knees, it hit me! The day had finally arrived!

"Today is my wedding day!" I exclaimed. That was very hard to believe.

The ceremony was to be held at six o'clock in the evening, but I was surprised about nine o'clock in the morning when I heard a car horn blowing in front of the house in the crisp winter weather. I couldn't believe my eyes when I looked out the window to see that it was my "husband to be" ALREADY — so early in the morning! My Aunt May told him that it was bad luck to see me before the wedding and she sent him home. I don't who was more anxious, him or me.

Both of us just wanted it to be over so we could be together, but away from all of the hubbub.

The time had finally come for me to put on my wedding dress. The lady who helped me get dressed, Roselee, was a very good friend of my Aunt May. At the time of this writing, she is still like part of the family. Roselee also helped Rosie put on her pretty little pink dress because she was my flower girl. As she was helping us get ready to walk down the stairs, my only regret was knowing that it was Cousin Charley who was going to give me away instead of my father.

[The biggest reason for this feeling was due to the fact that he had been making advances toward me. Believe it or not he had even tried it again on my wedding day.]

As I looked into the mirror and saw how pretty we looked in our beautiful dresses, I felt a deep sadness grip my heart because I knew that, when I walked down the stairs, Cousin Charley would be standing at the bottom of the steps, waiting to take my hand and walk me across the room where the groom would be waiting where he would "give me" to Arthur whether he really wanted to or not.

As I found myself daydreaming, contemplating this entire situation and its repercussions, I became very nervous. The more I thought about it, the more fearful I became. It took me a good half hour after I dressed to pull myself together enough to descend those stairs because I didn't want Cousin Charley to touch me nor did I want to stop the wedding. Roselee repeatedly reminded me that I had to go downstairs and that everyone was waiting for me. Suddenly I burst into tears at which time she began asking me again and again, "What's the matter? Why are you crying?"

I knew that I had to tell her something, but I didn't want to tell her the whole truth because I was too afraid. After all, I didn't really want to hurt the one person who had been so nice to me — my Aunt May. Finally, after being counseled and comforted by Roselee, I was able to gather enough courage to walk down what seemed like an endless flight of stairs as my little Sister led the way.

Sure enough, as I reached the bottom of the steps, there he was, just as I expected. As I looked into his eyes he seemed like another person; a person who was innocent of any wrongdoing. He acted as if nothing had ever happened between us. As I think back to that time, I can still visualize that funny grin on his face as we walked across the room. When the preacher asked, "Who gives this woman to be married to this man?" he let go of my arm and loudly said, "I do." At that time I felt as if I had been relieved of a gigantic burden. I was so glad to be standing next to Arthur, the man I was to marry. It was such a comfort to be next to him.

[I'd like to pause here and say a little bit about Arthur. He was tall, dark, and very, very handsome. He had dark, wavy hair. He was a very soft-spoken, gentle man. When he spoke, it was like something melted my heart because of his gentle nature.]

I felt so good just standing next to him! I just couldn't wait for my turn to say, "I do," because I knew that, without a shadow of a doubt, he was mine — a-a-l-l-l mine — because he was a "one-woman man."

As we exchanged our vows, it was a beautiful sight to behold, especially in my thoughts.

After the vows had been exchanged I was so thrilled as we pledged ourselves to each other "until death do us part," and the minister said, "I pronounce you man and wife. You may kiss the bride." Arthur then literally picked me up off of the floor and yelled, "My wife! My wife!" He couldn't stop wildly hugging me and squeezing me. Everybody was looking at us in awe. Oh, I was so embarrassed!

After we got ourselves and our emotions calmed down and under control, we went into the dining room with our guests and sat down at the pretty table which Aunt May had prepared. It was heavy laden with all sorts of delicious and colorful dishes of food. Some of the guests who were there included Dr. and Mrs. Ervin Hom and their children. Their presence meant something extra special to me because I hadn't been employed by them very long and they had shown me how much they thought of me by coming to my wedding.

"After all," I thought, "I am just another one of their workers."

As I contemplated their presence I suddenly realized that I was no longer in the deep South, but that I was able to freely mix with white people. The Home family was treating me differently than I'd ever been treated before — like a "real person," instead of a slave. I repeat, I was a genuine person to them a peer instead of a "black person." Skin color didn't seem to make any difference to them.

After the ceremony and the reception were over, we posed for photographs as "bride and groom. The bridal party," and other combinations of the bride and groom with some of our guests. I still have a picture of Arthur and me, pictured with the Homed family, my baby sister Rosie, and her friend Louise.

The reception finally ended about midnight when the last of the guests left, so Arthur and I left Cousin Charley's house and set out for our pretty little apartment which was in a private home on John Street in Elmira which was owned by Mrs. Woods. Mrs. Woods had fixed it up so that it looked just like a pretty little doll house, It was so precious — neat, sweet, dainty, and cute. I can still visualize it as I think about it.

As I think back on my wedding day and that beautiful little apartment, it makes me think of James 1:17 which says, "Every good ... and ... perfect gift is from above, and cometh down from the Father of lights, and I am reminded that He had led me beside the still waters and had restored my soul (Psalm 23:2, 3) even though I really didn't know Him as my Savior. In this moment I felt Joy!

You see, I believe that the Lord was watching over me even though I didn't truly "know Him" yet because He had called me, but I wasn't really listening, so I hadn't heard Him yet. I didn't know how to hear Him in spite of my many cries for help. Because of this, I had many more years of troubles, tears, difficult experiences, joy, and peace...These poems along with God's promises have continued to carry me through.

Step

By Barbara C. Ryberg

He does not lead me year by year
Nor even day by day.
But step by step my path unfolds:

Tomorrow's paths I do not know.
I only know this minute:

But He will say. "This is the way.
By faith now walk ye in it."

And I am glad that it is so.
Today's enough to bear:
And when tomorrow comes, His grace
Shall far exceed its care.

What need to worry then, or fret?
The God who gave His Son
Holds all my moments in His hand
And gives them, one by one.

Live Each Day to the Fullest

By Jean Kyler McManus

Yesterday's troubles are written in sand.
Brushed out of existence
By Gods' own hand –
The things of the future,
Our in hearts may fear.

Can all be resolved when tomorrow is here…

Out of a lifetime, these hours alone –
The hours of TODAY
Are completely our own…
So as each sun is setting
There's a reason to say.
"Thanks, Lord, for your gifts –
Above all, for this day."

Don't Carry the Burdens of Tomorrow

By "Anonymous"

God broke our years into hours and days,
That hour by hour, and day by day,
Just going on a little way,
We might be able, all along,
To keep quite strong.

Should all the weight of life be laid
Across our shoulders at just one place,
And the future, rife with woe and struggle,
Meet us face to face:
We could not go:
Our feet would stop, and so
God LAYS A LITTLE ON US EVERY DAY.

And never, I believe, in all life's way,
Will burdens bear so deep,
Or pathways lie so steep,
But we can go, if, by God's power,
WE ONLY BEAR THE BURDEN OF THE HOUR.

About the Author

Ruby Adams born February 16, 1938 lived her late teenage years into adulthood in Upstate, NY. Although she has lived the majority of her life in the North, this book memorializes her childhood experiences living in the Deep South of Georgia and how these experiences gave her understanding of God's powerful and unwavering love, before she truly came to fully understand his power over her life.

Ruby Adams known by many as Sister Ruby has been a member of The Seventh Day Adventist Church for fifty plus years. She has been a devout member teaching, speaking, ministering, and spreading God's love within her community and to all those in which she encounters. Her objective is to share with her readers a small piece of her life story to encourage them and express to them how God's love supersedes all.

Have you ever been in a situation where you are wondering why or how, or feel down and out about your situation, to sit back one day and feel happy and at peace and still wonder why or how you got to such a place of joy…Ruby conveys the answer through her own personal journey and struggles….Doesn't Anybody Hear My Cry?

Letter from Your Namesake

Dear Grams: It is with joy in my heart that I write this letter to you. I am honored and privileged that you entrusted me to finalize this project for you. At this moment you are almost 83 years of age and I wanted to share how proud I am of you. Your unwavering Godly love not only guided you through life but has guided me as well. I am eternally grateful for the lessons and stories that you have shared; that now allow me to be the wife and mother that God has called me to be. You are my hero and I am thankful to also be named, Ruby. May God's Blessings continue to pour over you as you continue to manifest and share his greatness over us and all those that you encounter. In Jesus Name!

Forever your grand-daughter,
Little Ruby